nature's way

DESIGNING THE LIFE YOU WANT THROUGH THE LENS OF NATURE AND THE FIVE SEASONS

KARYN PRENTICE

"One touch of nature makes the whole world kin"

Shakespeare: *Troilus and Cressida Act 3, Scene 3*

ISBN: 978-1-9162-5050-5

Cover design and interior formatting by Andy Meaden / meadencreative.com

permissions

The author acknowledges and expresses her gratitude to the following for permission to reproduce their work in this book:

Sam Magill for the poems 'Yes' on page 71 and 'Harvest Timing' on page 246, from collected poems *Fully Human* (2006) Balcladdoch Press, Edmonds, Washington.

Denise Levertov for 'Stepping Westwards' on page 97 from *Poems 1960-1967*.

'You Shall Ask' © 1974 Nancy C. Wood on on page 144, reprinted from *Many Winters*; 'The Fire of Life' © 1998 Nancy C. Wood on pages 83 and 102, reprinted from *Sacred Fire*. Courtesy of the Nancy Wood Literary Trust www.NancyWood.com

To Peter
The heart and soul of my garden

contents

foreword
our superpower, growth

At the end of 2016, I found myself at an interesting juncture in my professional life. It felt personal because my professional life has always been tied up with my values and identity. This, set against the backdrop of the turmoil and political shift in the UK and the rest of the world, made for uncertainty in both a micro and macro sense. And yet, and yet, I felt the power and presence of *change* all around me – a shifting landscape both internally and externally.

As with all periods of change, there were growing pains but there were also glorious moments of hope, of optimism, and of the possibility of a new and different future.

When I began my journey to try and create a new future for myself, I knew that I needed someone who would not only coach me to ask the questions of myself that needed to be asked, but also someone who would inspire me, guide me; someone who would encourage me and walk beside me in my journey of change and growth. This someone came in the form of a coach, a wonderful and skilled woman called Karyn. We met every six to eight weeks on Skype. The power of these meetings was transformative. Using the metaphor of the internal garden and the force of nature with its ever changing and growing cycles, Karyn inspired me and skilfully encouraged me to visualise the garden of my life that I wanted to cultivate.

In Haemin Sunim's wonderful book, *The Things You Can See Only When You Slow Down,* he tells a story of the Buddhist scripture, *The Lotus Sutra.* A Buddha makes a prophecy that 500 disciples will achieve the final stage of Buddhahood and, hearing his belief in them, they do. Haemin shares a story of his own, which also illustrates the same point about a teacher who encouraged him in such a way that it made him work harder towards his own future: 'One word of encouragement said with kindness and hope can change a person's future.' Just as the Buddha's words inspired growth in his disciples, so encouragement can change the course of a life.

My own experience chimed so clearly with this; the teacher who inspires us to set off on a particular path, or someone we meet in later life who has a profound and lasting impact on who we are.

In *Nature's Way,* Karyn draws on the wisdom of nature to encourage us to look to the cycle of the seasons, to create the garden of our life now and for the future.

I remember one of the very first questions that Karyn asked of me: 'What will have grown in the next three years, and what needs to make way for that growth?' She invited me to borrow some of my young daughter's coloured pens and to draw a garden, however crudely, and in it to include elements that represented different aspects of my life in the present. Then I was to re-create the garden as I wanted it to be three years later and see what needed to be pruned along the way to make way for new growth.

Using some of the techniques that are outlined in *Nature's Way,* I discovered unexplored corners of my internal garden. When I started the process, I was surprised by the things that came up for me. Long-ago forgotten dreams surfaced like the first small buds of Spring, hope dawned like a fresh day and I recognised knotty challenges like gnarled dead wood that needed to be burnt because actually it was no longer going to be of any use in the garden of my future self.

In an age where so many people are finally beginning to truly appreciate the crucial relationship that humans have with nature, at a time when more people than ever turn to the natural world for inspiration and clarity, *Nature's Way* is a valuable and relevant resource that is as accessible as it is beautifully written. 2019 has seen the birth of the incredible movement, *Extinction Rebellion,* a global movement led by the people, one that recognises our pivotal relationship to the environment and how we all need to work together to save the planet. If ever there was a time to become more aware of and more engaged with the force of nature and all its inherent magic, it is now.

Today, almost three years later, the cycle has progressed and nearly everything I foresaw for my future has come to pass. I find I am more alive to the shifting seasons and my relationship to them, both internally and externally. Changes I made during the time I worked with Karyn have helped me to make my life richer and at the same time to appreciate more fully what my life is.

Nature's Way is a timely manual for those of us seeking to live a life that is more in tune with the seasons and with the ever-changing cycles of not only the natural world but of our own lives. In it, Karyn generously shares moments from her own life that have led her to write such an extraordinary book. These passages are lyrical and steeped in beautiful images and observations of the natural world. The sections that offer exercises and the process of using the way of nature to create change are accessible, engaging and ultimately life-changing.

This book is a humble invitation to anyone who wishes to change their lives, to anyone who is willing to become more attuned to the alchemy of the natural world, and to adventurers and explorers everywhere to set off on a journey of discovery and transformation.

Natasha Carlish

Centre Director for The Hurst, The John Osborne Arvon Centre

July 2019

preface
the rhythms of nature

Whenever I go back to my native California in the United States, as soon as I step out of the airport, I stop for a few moments and just look up. The azure blue sky and palm tree silhouettes, each with their lion's ruff of brown, shaggy leaves at the base, remind me of my childhood. Everything may have changed since then but this aerial view is still there. Instantly, I am transported back to summers lying on the grass, my ten-year-old arms spread horizontally as I daydreamed about travelling to imaginary lands. Where I grew up, the seasons were not so distinct; we had plenty of sunshine much of the year. It was easy to take the hundreds of blue-sky days for granted. Days were warm from morning until evening, when temperatures would take a strong dip. In the distant hills, from our street I could see the iconic Hollywood sign, bright white against the hillside cradle it sat on. Rain was infrequent. At school, every day we ate our paper bag lunches as we sat outside on wooden benches and tables.

I looked forward to Autumn when the leaves turned into a palette of golden tones and hues. It would be a chance, by late November at least, to wear pullovers and sweaters in the season's traditional colours of russet, olive, antique gold, sienna brown, and what I call a faux yellow, meaning it wasn't a true yellow but rather a melange of speckled tones of summer green fading into an orangey copper.

I liked playing outside even when it felt cold. Once in a sweater and maybe a coat, I was fascinated by the steam of my warm breath meeting sharp coldness as I roller skated or cycled until I came indoors to warm up and have a hot drink. When school holidays began the summers seemed endless. My friend Elissa and I invented games and often we were outside from morning till suppertime. We pretended we were wild ponies. We made imaginary campsites. We designed and made game and puzzle books for each other. We went for long walks on Saturday afternoons. Nature was always the backdrop to the theatre of our adventures as we wandered the radius of two neighbourhoods and out along the circumference of our local world. Our imagination turned Nature into a range of circus props: trees were climbing frames, bushes a place to tie up imaginary steeds, and secret paths could be discovered through interlinking back gardens. We laughed a lot. I remember one time laughing so hard, the hot chocolate I had been drinking came out of my nose. I could feel the smarting sensation in my nostrils for a long time afterwards. Sixty years later, we still talk about those days.

I was only a little more than 16 when my life changed forever. One morning I went off to school waving goodbye to my Dad and that same afternoon, a friend drove me from school to the hospital to collect my mother, now a widow at 46. She was so devastated she never found her equilibrium again, such was her grief. Three months later, an only child with no other family, I buried my mother too. A cold became pneumonia and within days she was gone. What kept me going on a daily basis was that I was lucky enough to have a small circle of loved ones, exceptionally bighearted parents of my best friend, who were brave enough to take me on, love me and believe in me so that I could carry on my daily life and school routine.

Besides this blessing, I also needed a wider kind of holding and sense of ground beneath me as I learned to adjust to my changed life circumstances. Nature felt like the only container large enough to hold all my feelings, which were too jumbled to iterate or too frozen to have formed into much more than the howl of abandonment. The pain of loss showed up as an exquisite numbness that appeared and disappeared like a slowly flashing light on an empty street; now there, now gone, now there, now gone. Being outdoors soothed me and reminded me in an impersonal way that there was a dependable regular rhythm that was far bigger than me. Nature was like a giant lap that held me as I railed, wept, and survived. Looking up at those seemingly unrelenting blue skies and swaying palms was an almost spiritual experience.

Life went on. Magnolia and oleander continued to blossom. Poinsettias grew to full size. All around there were orange trees in people's gardens. My next door neighbour had fig and avocado trees so laden with fruit they frequently dropped, overcome by their sheer weight and size. This richness spilled out around me and I could lean into it. And I could keep going.

Wild California poppies dotted the hills, as did Californian fuchsia with its scarlet flowers. In contrast, tall colonies of agave with its tooth-like thorns and paddle shapes stood like sentinels at attention, soaking up the hot sunshine. Our garden, though small and relatively sparse, had chalk live-forever with their succulent rosettes that began way back then my love of all succulents.

There was hummingbird sage, its fragrance seducing the beautiful ephemeral hummingbirds to drink from the flowers. I would sit as still as I could and watch these miniature birds come to a feeder attached to the big kitchen window. Weighing less than a five pence coin, the hummingbirds would hover in the air, their tiny wings moving so quickly they didn't even seem like wings but more tiny propellers framing their iridescent pinky-green tiny breast feathers as they drank the sugar water or dipped their beaks into the flower's trumpet buds.

Every morning I checked for the daily appearance of morning glories with their purple or white trumpets. When flowers and fruit disappeared, others took their place. Autumn was replaced by a short Winter, then it was Spring again. All these anchor points helped me in my own coping system as I transitioned from a parentless young person to an independent and strong young adult.

The harvest festivals of fruits and vegetables, pumpkins and squashes, tomatoes and other crops at the county fairs celebrated the abundance of the land, which was a triumph then over the constant battle for enough water. The dryness that lies beneath Southern California's greenness is desert. Water had to be diverted from elsewhere to support the lushness. Even that iconic palm tree is an early 20th century import. For me, it meant that whatever the conditions, Nature, together with the appropriate and due care of humankind, could grow something spectacular. It just took time.

I would get in my car and drive out of the city most weekends, month after month. Unlike the short blocks where I lived, the streets out there could run for miles. Sunset Boulevard is 22 miles long and moves from concentrated downtown fizz to suburban greenery to opulent hillside homes and finally to the Pacific Ocean. I needed the open space and the time by myself. Windows rolled down and anticipating the ozone smell of the ocean air or the scrubby bush of headlands, all those variations smelt and felt welcoming. I would walk, sit, read, write, grieve and eat Cap'n Crunch cereal straight from the box (my unique 'drug of choice'). In the early days of the hippie movement, there I was sitting on a mountain top with my journal and a family size box of cereal.

I took myself to a meditation centre perched high above the Pacific Coast Highway facing Malibu. Called the Self Realization Centre, it was a haven of peace and calm, a refuge where I returned regularly to bask in the green, the sky, the water and the mountains season after season.

It took me many years to be able to articulate how powerful a nurturing influence this seasonal regularity was as I sat with my journal, week after week, after school or at weekends. It was my therapy as I walked, sat and began to come to terms with my loss. It kept me hopeful of having hope.

After I graduated from high school, I applied and was accepted to a college in France. It was the right thing for me. Even though I never went back to live in the United States, I wouldn't be the person I am today without the experience of growing up there and having the reservoir of love and support of the wonderful family that made me one of theirs when I had no more family of my own.

Since then, for over 45 years, I have lived mainly in the UK. With a business career in London, I also became a psychotherapist, a coach and a coaching supervisor. I have spent years leading and facilitating development groups, working with individuals in their chosen fields, from individual artists to educators in higher and further education in the UK and in other countries, and with organisations of all kinds and backgrounds. I also worked with people on personal issues who were trying to make sense of their lives in different ways.

The ideas, material and approaches I share in this book show up throughout my work and in my own learning and growth. I began to join all these strands by weaving Nature as a companion, partner and 'inspiratrice' into the generative conversation of inquiry, reflection and personal insight.

For decades I watched my husband be everything a gardener needs to be: patient, optimistic, realistic, supple, pragmatic and generous. His skills have produced glorious creations as if from nowhere. He has waited stalwartly for a brown twig to ignite into life time and time again. It has been a great influence on the connection I make between the dedicated attention he brings to the garden, year on year, and the work I do with people.

As a pragmatic sort of soul, I like the simplicity of gardening language because it serves as an excellent metaphor for viewing our own life as a personal garden, in order to help us flourish. For instance, the concept of not overfilling a pot so that plants can breathe applies as well to how it can be easy to overfill your own life and have no space left to manoeuvre with ease, and to making sure the soil you plant bulbs or seedlings in contains the nutrients compatible with the growing conditions required. The gardens and parks we walk in or visit all lend themselves to a metaphorical one; the garden that is our life itself. Whether we compost, seed, or double dig our back garden, all these activities translate into a useful lens through which to view our daily lives. We seed ideas, plans and projects. We need to tend to the roots and soil of who we are in order to grow into our potential. Like an acorn that over time becomes a strong and beautiful oak tree, we have inside of us what it takes to be fully who we can be. What we do and who we are has its own rhythmic cycles.

This book was planted in the soil of that reflection, enriched by and in service to all the people I have worked with for over 30 years. People who have been brave and courageous and daring enough to reach for new goals, live with tough decisions and develop new ways of being and doing, deepening their relationships to themselves and to others. I am eternally grateful to have been trusted by them. I have been endlessly amazed at what people can accomplish and never surprised at how much more treasure is in each of us.

My hope is that this book becomes a companion guide, tucked into a backpack, thumbed through and revisited until it is a bit 'spludgy' and 'foldy' from repeated readings. Whether you intend to connect with the spirit of each season in order to discover new territory within yourself or in your own life garden, or simply appreciate what is right here beneath your feet right now, this book adds value.

Because this seasonal cycle moves through the entire year, it is designed to take 12 months to complete. This is not a fast book, to be devoured within a few days. It is a companion book, to be kept by your bedside and accompany you on your walks in Nature. Take your time and enjoy.

Nature's Way brings the language of the garden to the journey of our lives today and throughout the seasons. It represents a deep bow of gratitude to Nature. We need only turn towards it with an open heart and mind and a willingness to wander inside and out. There is a garden in you already waiting to flourish.

how to use this book
preparing for the journey

If you have picked up this book it is probably because, in the garden of your life, something is calling you to take some time and bide awhile. Take some time to sit and marvel, puzzle and identify what is working well and what might need a fresh approach.

To get the most out of this book there are some requisites: scooting over and making some time and space within which to reflect that you can ring-fence from all the other demands upon your daily life. You may need to negotiate with yourself, your diary and maybe with others in your life to scoop out some 'me' time for yourself in which to reflect, write, walk and explore the various activities in this book.

The activities are varied and can be spaced out over several weeks or even months. Part 1 of the book, The Five Seasons, is divided into the five seasons of Winter, Spring, Summer, Late Summer and Autumn, and although they may follow the same structure, the activities in each section are tailored to each specific season and the content will vary accordingly. Regular practices like mindfulness, journaling, and seasonal walks will enrich and enliven what is already in the garden of your life or inspire you to envisage and create more of the garden and life that you want.

You will get the most from this book if you can devote a minimum of 15 minutes a day or an hour a week to the exercises and activities suggested. If you can manage more, you will see the difference. However, it should fit in with your life so that it becomes a welcome addition to everyday life rather than an intrusion.

Before you begin, I suggest you treat yourself to a blank page book or journal. Blank because it gives you the maximum space to write or draw or stick a photo in, and may feel less reminiscent of school.

Pick something that you really like because it will be your regular companion over the course of working through this book. Your journal may be something you come back to a year or more along the way. It seems to me that shops and stores are stocking more and more blank book journals, from the corporate-looking plain and sleek Moleskine, to varied and colourful journals to suit all pockets and choices. Even supermarkets stock some lovely ones now. Writing by hand, compared to typing on a keyboard, has a kinaesthetic benefit, which is of itself a resourcing tool and an aid to reflective writing by slowing us down a bit. It is a way to be more present as we connect head and heart ideas to paper as a grounding exercise. It is also an opportunity to take a break from the digital world many of us live and work in. If you feel that you cannot possibly write by hand, then of course a tablet option is fine – though I encourage keeping a pen and paper handy as well, just in case.

Nature's Way invites you to bring four qualities and skills to bear throughout this book: **compassion**, **patience**, **mindful awareness** and **reflection**.

Begin your journey in the current season in which you start reading. This will invite you into a more intimate alignment with the natural world right in front of you by inviting you to tune in to present moment **mindful awareness**. This is an opportunity to engage with greater acuity with the season and with yourself just as things are right now.

This book is about giving yourself some non-judgemental loving kindness and **self-compassion** while also bringing a sense of curiosity and wonder to exploring the known and unknown. Nature can't always be rushed at the behest of humankind. Seasons have their cycles and so do we.

Patience is required to temper the desire to race to get to the end of this book. Getting to the end is not the purpose of the journey or of this book. The benefit in slowing down is to be present to a deeper gratitude for and appreciation of what is right now.

To take all that you harvest from the book, at various points there will be an invitation to pause and reflect. These **'Greenhousing points'** are provided to support you in capturing your own insights in the moment and allowing them time and space to evolve. They help you to digest your learning and see what resonates personally in your life and your story. A greenhouse is where we put tender plants to be protected against the buffeting of extreme weather while they grow. Sometimes, new thinking territories we explore can feel tender as well.

Reflection helps us take time to explore, to ponder and not jump too quickly into full-blown action. Your reading will mirror the outdoor world. If you are living somewhere outside of your usual season, in another part of the world, that will also bring interesting insights for you to reflect on. You could explore the garden on your own or you might enlist a friend who is equally keen to explore, someone who can be your garden buddy for a year.

Each season is important and overall is part of an interlocking cycle of life, death and rebirth. Honouring what each offers is a way to reflect creatively about what is happening in our own lives or in the organisations within which we work.

This book will serve you best if you make a commitment to yourself to get outdoors to do some of the exercises, even if it means just standing outside the backdoor or on a balcony, so Nature is more than a concept, but a felt sense too. The result can be a deeply moving, very personal way to redefine what is important in life, to increase our awareness and to draw upon our innate wisdom about what we can do to make our garden flourish.

Postcards from the Hedgerow is a feature that appears at the end of each season's chapter. It offers a range of creative and reflective exercises, shaped as weekly walks, which encourage you to get outdoors, and to make an initimate link between what you see and experience, and who you are and want to be. In Nature, hedgerows can be made of lots of different bush types, wild shrubs or low trees bordering a field or lane. They help keep woods naturally diverse and provide an important habitat for animals and plants, act as boundaries for fields and can help modify environmental conditions.

For our purposes here, we want to be aware and connected to our own internal landscape by paying more attention in the moment. So before setting out on your weekly walk, we can prepare.

A standard postcard is a simple, portable place to capture a flash of insight, or a moment to remember in a year's time. You might choose to capture something you saw, sensed or experienced as you walked. You may have some old unused postcards sitting in drawers in your home right now. Or you can copy the simple vintage one on the next page. Pop one in your pocket, backpack or bag with a pen or pencil before you set off for your walk. At some point during or after your walk use the card to do some bitesize journaling. It is not too daunting a space to fill. You may even decide to continue writing in a journal later. However, the fresh, in-the-moment jotting is a good way to take in the goodness and digest it a little bit further. After following the cycle over 12 months, you will have a wonderful collection of personal postcards from your walks.

"We all travel the Milky Way together, trees and men ... In every walk with nature one receives far more than he seeks. The clearest way into the universe is through a forest wilderness"

John Muir

PART 1
the five seasons

CHAPTER 1
introducing the five seasons

"To everything there is a season and a time to every purpose under heaven"

Ecclesiastes 3:1

Cycles of the seasons

The season cycle is made up of five parts. Besides Spring, Summer, Autumn and Winter, Late Summer is included here in the exploration of the seasons, falling between Summer and Autumn. Together, they can be viewed as a cycle of birth, growth, ripeness, harvest, gratitude, pruning and letting go, reflecting, and germinating for new birth and possibilities.

Every season has its own particular energy, essence or beauty. Depending on where you live, you may experience some seasons more vividly than others. One season might speak to you more than another. At the same time, each season can be experienced as a mirror, reflecting our own cycles of internal motivations and energies, inviting us to find connections between what we notice outside in Nature and what we experience inside of us in our inner nature.

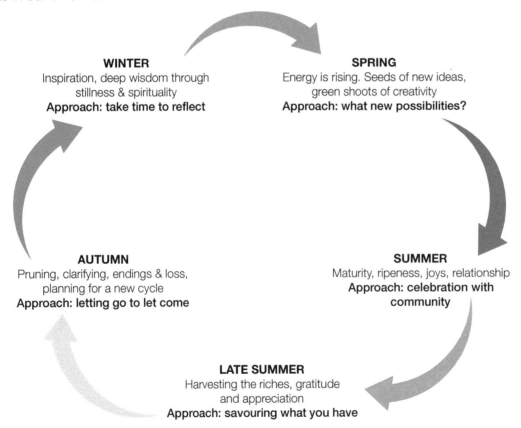

WINTER
Inspiration, deep wisdom through stillness & spirituality
Approach: take time to reflect

SPRING
Energy is rising. Seeds of new ideas, green shoots of creativity
Approach: what new possibilities?

AUTUMN
Pruning, clarifying, endings & loss, planning for a new cycle
Approach: letting go to let come

SUMMER
Maturity, ripeness, joys, relationship
Approach: celebration with community

LATE SUMMER
Harvesting the riches, gratitude and appreciation
Approach: savouring what you have

As in any cycle, there are phases and these phases repeat and we begin again. As a teacher, Nature offers us a chance to learn from the characteristics of each season and the part they play in the whole cycle. Even if we live in a country where the seasons may not be as sharply distinctive as they are in other parts of the world, we can still use this language to grow and develop. It invites us into a reflective practice about our own inner seasons and weather and what we need in order to flourish. We give ourselves the gift of nurturing the ground and roots of who we really are.

We can get closer to the themes and patterns that arise in our own life or work cycles as much as those that arise in the garden, year on year. In my garden I learn, sometimes through hard lessons of repetition, that some plants do better in certain places and some don't do well at all in the soil we have. I can enrich the soil in many cases, move certain plants to different spots or I can try a different plant that can adapt and thrive where it is. If I don't pay attention, some plants will die. Some will die back only to reappear next year stronger than ever. Other times I might be quite surprised that out of the blue, a plant appears because a bird dropped a seed on its way through my garden in Autumn.

For many years I have delighted in drawing upon the universal language of the seasons in my work with people, inviting the essence and qualities of each season to illuminate inquiry and discovery. As we walk and talk together outdoors, the season we are in provides a creative lens through which to view and reflect on what arises, teasing out fresh perspectives and relevant connections.

The Five Season cycle is a metaphor for exploring issues that interest and concern us. The seasons can inform our thinking and feeling as we reflect on what we need to move through life with courage, joy and compassion in ways that resource us and help us flourish in every season.

While we experience the seasons in Nature throughout a calendar year, we can also experience the cycle in miniature over a single day, for example, or over an entire lifetime. Too much or too little of any part of the cycle has an impact on the cycle as a whole. Sometimes when we get stuck it's because we have not taken sufficient heed of what is needed in each part of the cycle so that we can have optimal functioning. As the writer Laurence Durrell says '…you do not need a sixth sense for it. It is there if you just close your eyes and breathe softly through your nose; you will hear the whispered message, for all landscapes ask the same question in the same whisper. "I am watching you – are you watching yourself in me?"'[1]

The seasons call us to heed our own inner ecology as well as how we show up in the world. We can always gain a greater appreciation of the elements that both subtly and dynamically inform our ebb and flow. We attune to where we may need to address imbalances with a bit more compassion, whether it is adding a bit more 'Winter' of slowing down and reflecting, bringing more 'Late Summer' savouring to what we have right now, or topping up on 'Spring' energy to boost our vitality.

This part of the book explores each of the Five Seasons in turn. We begin with an overview of each season's essence, and the qualities and practices associated with it. This sequence is repeated in each season, with exercises, walks, visualisations, stories and reflective questions. Accompanying case studies show how attention to the qualities of a particular season can help us with various aspects of our life and work. All the materials are designed to ignite, or refresh, your relationship to the particular season and promote creative entry points into reflecting on what matters most to you.

Begin this section by immersing yourself in the season you find yourself in now, so that the chapter you are reading mirrors the essence of Nature around you. The end of each chapter features a section called **Postcards from the Hedgerow.** These offer prompts to take you through the weeks of that season and accompany you on a walk in Nature once a week. Choose the questions that call to you most strongly. Listen to your inner knowing. Keep a log of your experiences in your journal, including key words and phrases that arise in your reflections, or photos or drawings that you capture as you walk. Create a postcard for each walk so that after a year you will have a unique record of your own Five Seasons.

"We are water. We are air. We grow, we bloom, we seed, we wilt, we die. There is a false separation between humanity and nature"

Nora Bateson, Small Arcs of Larger Circles

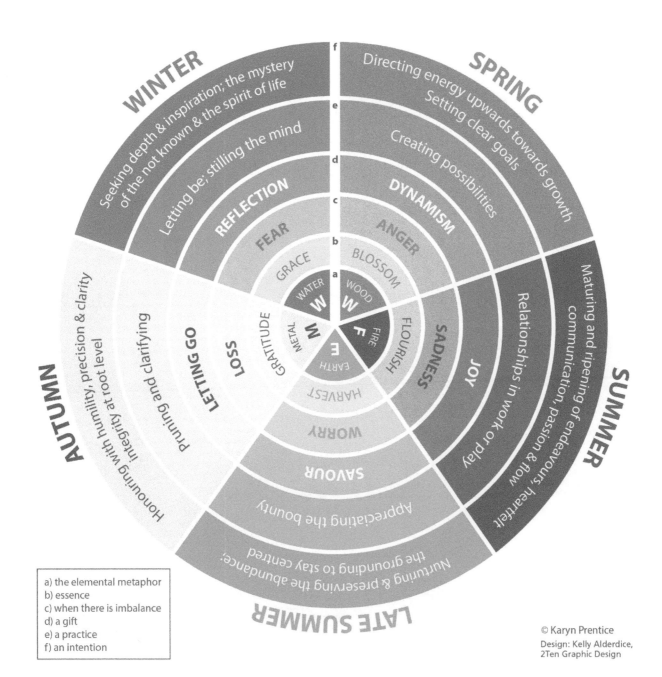

The five seasons wheel:

WINTER — WATER
- Seeking depth & inspiration; the mystery of the not known & the spirit of life
- Letting be; stilling the mind
- REFLECTION
- FEAR
- GRACE
- WATER / W

SPRING — WOOD
- Directing energy upwards towards growth
- Setting clear goals
- Creating possibilities
- DYNAMISM
- ANGER
- BLOSSOM
- WOOD / W

SUMMER — FIRE
- Maturing and ripening of endeavours; heartfelt communication, passion & now
- Relationships in work or play
- JOY
- SADNESS
- FLOURISH
- FIRE / F

LATE SUMMER — EARTH
- Nurturing & preserving the abundance; the grounding to stay centred
- Appreciating the bounty
- SAVOUR
- WORRY
- HARVEST
- EARTH / E

AUTUMN — METAL
- Honouring with humility, precision & clarity; integrity at root level
- Pruning and clarifying
- LETTING GO
- LOSS
- GRATITUDE
- METAL / M

Legend:
a) the elemental metaphor
b) essence
c) when there is imbalance
d) a gift
e) a practice
f) an intention

© Karyn Prentice
Design: Kelly Alderdice,
2Ten Graphic Design

CHAPTER 2
winter

I am standing in my conservatory, both hands wrapped around a duck-egg blue crockery mug of steaming, pungent coffee. It is nearly full to the brim and the yellow lining of my mug is almost covered by tan froth. I love the smell of a strong, dark brew, anticipating the first taste waiting just beneath the fluffy surface. I know it is going to be good and its nutty, subtle aroma invites a little hum from me, joining with the purr of my cat who sits, Zen-like, to my left. I have been trying to come up with some new ideas and have reached a mental roadblock. So taking a break is a good thing at this point. Standing here, I survey the now almost monochrome garden in front of me. My ideas bank for the moment is also monochrome. I am having a mental 'Winter' moment, which is coinciding with the season outdoors.

I can see the intrepid robin, little legs akimbo, who makes his base camp in one of the garden borders. Unlike many birds, the robin begins to sing from January. Our robin, I imagine, is thinking about a late breakfast this January morning... The grass is slick with night rain. The hoary frost of the last few days has given way to a weak but welcome flush of winter sun. The usual neighbourhood weekday morning noise of cars and school buses has dispersed and there is a peaceful calm outside. My garden is not at its prettiest right now by any means, yet what I love most about this season are three things.

First of all, I love watching the garden sleeping. The bareness of branches reveals the sculpture of the trees, like lithe, lean dancers in a range of vertical poses. I like the hazel with its curly branches. I wonder what evolved in its DNA so long ago that its survival depended on becoming curly. It can be easy to dismiss the garden and landscape at this time of the year. It is cold, often wet, and maybe snowy or icy. For me, this sparseness has grace pared down to its essence.

Second, a lot of what makes my garden beautiful in the Spring and Summer is what happens underground in Winter. I like the fanciful notion that my tulip bulbs are gently snoring beneath the trees and lawn with their inner alarm clocks set for quarter past spring.

Third, I appreciate the invitation to be in a silent and still space as an intrinsic part of the cycle of renewal – for myself as well as the garden. Even if it is part of a mini-cycle of renewal in a single day, it is as vital to human flourishing as it is to the garden. Standing here with my coffee, I take a little pause to enjoy it. The robin and I both survey the garden for our own needs. I know that I am refuelling myself by taking this brief time today to be fully present. Attending to my own inner microclimate has made all the difference and now I am ready to crack on.

For some years now the value of slowing down, stopping, and being in the present moment has grown in awareness in a big way. Fast can be good, but fast can also miss the point. We can only be physically present in this very moment. As you read these words on the page I hope you are one hundred percent here as you read. Our minds easily drift to what might have been or could still happen. Before an experience has ended we want to fast-forward to the next.

Cycles within cycles

Winter in the cycle is a time to resource ourselves in a deeper, soulful, or spiritual way. To go deep and be still for a while is part of regeneration before the bloom and green shoots of fresh starts in Spring, and then the joyful arrival of peak moments of full-on Summer success, both in ourselves and with others. In a metaphorical sense, these cycles happen not just over a year, but over a month, or even a day. Our recognition of them means we can appreciate and make the most of the ebb and flow.

Now we are moving into Winter's energy. In Winter we can allow ourselves to pause or stop, however briefly, and take a deep dive into who we are in our deeper selves, in the way that most suits us. We need the courage to be there and listen with a finely tuned ear to the note that tells us who we truly are. This is saluting the Higher Self in ourselves. Carl Jung, in his *Collected Works,*[2] writes about the transpersonal part of ourselves that is beyond or 'more than' the sum of all the roles we play; hence the word 'trans': the everyday self that goes about daily life. It is the part of us that feels the hairs on the back of our neck tingle when we hear music that truly moves us, or see a gorgeous sunset or something that connects us with the very mystery of life itself. This has a different timbre than the everyday self that gets on with the business of daily life; it is our spiritual or soulful Self, with a capital 'S'. We may only experience it as a fleeting moment or it may be something that we are deeply familiar with. It connects us with something bigger, deeper and universal, perhaps. The mystery of life is always available if we take the time to be gentle with ourselves and find a quiet place to listen from the heart to this note that is ours and ours alone.

Like plants, we humans need time to incubate ideas, plans, projects, and note what needs time and patience to emerge in the next season. This is nourishment from a deeper, unseen place. Our ability to be with ourselves and to rest in being and non-doing is hard in a world that measures patience by seconds and minutes. We are in continual movement, change and doing that can feel relentless. Giving ourselves time to do this is a radical act of kindness and love for the person we are. This is a time for choosing to take some time out from 'doing' to a time of 'being'. Often the best ideas can emerge when we turn our direct attention away from them and let them germinate.

When we can also let ourselves experience this non-doing with greater awareness, we can draw upon imagination, intuition, perseverance and patience. In a world filled with ambiguity and uncertainty there are times when we may need to adjust our ability to be with these emotions in a different way, when certainty cannot be claimed by anyone. It is not a 'giving up' place. Going straight from A to B is a direct route. But it is not the only route. Some routes require us to meander, turn and curve before the best solution becomes apparent. Both direct and indirect ways of operating are valid. They draw on different preferences. In Chinese tradition they are referred to as yin (feminine energy) and yang (masculine energy).

Cultivating the art of 'letting be' is a Winter practice. Anxiety can result from anticipating what may or may not happen in the future or thinking about what has happened in the past. We may play it over again and again in the futile hope that a better version of the past might present itself. It is important to learn from yesterday and to take on board the learning. We can influence, plan for and be prepared to a certain degree for the future. But one thing is sure – we can only be present in this moment, right here, today. If we miss this moment, we miss the gift of life.

I remember as a child watching my mother plant tiny carrot seedlings in our garden. I was instantly fascinated by the idea that a tiny plant went in, and fully fledged large carrots emerged like magic. The one thing I found hard was waiting for the carrot to grow. After a few weeks, which seemed like an eternity to me as a child, I would gently tug on top of one of the miniature plants, only to be disappointed that there still was very little to show. Each time I waited a bit more, I would 'test' again by tugging on another plant, only for a tiny, dolly-size carrot to show itself. My mother must have known it was me or presumed some delicate little animal was selecting a green top on a regular basis – but in the end no carrots made their way to full growth that season.

"It is not a matter of letting go – you would if you could. Instead of 'let it go' we should probably say 'let it be'"

Jon Kabat-Zinn

Qualities associated with Winter

Inner wisdom

Spirituality

Dreams and mystery

Setting limits

Hibernation

Reflection and introspection

Stillness/silence

Metaphor and imagery

Death, the unknown

Shadow

Deep strength and potential

Capacity to persevere and be patient

Courage in adversity

Listening to the still small voice within

Grace

The role of elements in the Five Seasons

In traditional Chinese wisdom, *Wu Hsing*[3] is regarded as a dynamic, interdependent conceptual scheme of 'five phases' or elements: earth, fire, metal, wood and water wisdom. At the heart of it is the notion that human beings are part of Nature. Each of us is a container of endless gifts that can be brought to life through our own unique way of being, doing and speaking. As a series of metaphors, these gardening terms can at the same time describe being like a tree or a seed and that we are Spring, or Winter, signifying that we can be in Nature but also that we *are* Nature, a part of this wonderful landscape in which all life unfolds. The garden has its own annual cycle as the seasons follow each other. And so do we. Birth is followed by growth, moving into maturity, then to decline and return to the earth. So it is with all things. This can be seen as the intrinsic ability of life to regenerate itself and give birth to new life over and over again. This is gardening of the soul soil.

Winter and the element of water

In Chinese tradition, the element of **water** is associated with Winter. Water takes many shapes and textures. It can be soft, hard, icy, snowy, still, and flowing. It goes over, under and in-between. It is often thought of as a symbol of birth and rebirth. In a clear pool we see our own reflection. Water is also thought of as symbolically encouraging inner calm, regeneration and renewal that helps us be ready to jump into action in the Spring. Sometimes rushing madly, the force of water can be overpowering. When it is too much, or arrives too quickly, then water can be destructive. Without any movement at all, water can become stagnant. It can be frothy and lively as it crashes to shore at the ocean's edge. It can flow from great heights to arrive at quiet pools many metres down a mountain. So it is also about our own capacity to be in flow, to be raging, to be deep, and to be icy.

In every season in Nature, water is important. It balances the heat and dryness of Summer. It helps feed the earth and plants that allow for new growth in Spring. In the garden of life our daily, monthly, yearly cycle needs the deep waters of stillness as much as the waves of activity. Finding the balance between feeling resourced and feeling drained is often a knife-edge. Water links us to really listening deeply to our deepest self.

The essence of Winter

In the garden of life, the essence of Winter stems from qualities of stillness and reflection. Winter invites us to trust the emergence of insight and wisdom that is already within us when we take the space and time to reflect, dream and consider the deeper questions that are under the surface of everyday life, which we might not otherwise, in our busy lives, make time for.

Cultivating patience

In Winter we set our intention to dip deeply into knowing ourselves a little more and connecting to who we really are, to our meaning and purpose and even our deepest longing. This journey into ourselves does not require us to do very much more than cultivate the patience to still ourselves.

The practice of stilling the mind and 'letting be', without the business of having to fix, find solutions, resolve, plan, or be in action mode can be challenging. People often ask 'What are you doing these days?' rather than 'How are you being these days?' On the other hand, you may have a regular mindfulness or meditation practice you use throughout the year. These could be said to offer mini-moments of Winter energy. Here, in the full season of Winter, is the invitation to bide a bit longer so that we can reflect on the big questions like 'Who am I? What is really important right now, this year and for next?' There are many resources that can help us. One exceptional resource is Elaine Patterson's book *Reflect to Create,* which offers myriad ways to explore and build personal reflective practices. Winter invites us to trust the emergence of insight and wisdom when we take space and time to reflect, dream and sit with the deeper questions that are under the surface of everyday, busy living, which we might not otherwise make time for. For this, patience is very helpful, as is self-compassion.

I remember a breakfast cereal advertisement when I was a child that showed children eating a cooked cereal breakfast and then going off to school with the image of a glowing hearth inside their tummies to see them through the morning. In Winter, the image of the fire in the hearth is a symbolic one of home, warmth and return. It conjures for me tending our own inner hearth that we can come back to again and again, particularly through the shorter days and longer nights.

The Irish poet John O'Donohue writes in *Anam Cara,* 'there is a labyrinth in the soul'.[4]

To walk a labyrinth we must slow down and patiently make our way. In English we make a distinction between a labyrinth and a maze. A maze may have a number of blind alleys and blocked paths. In a labyrinth, there is only one way in that takes us to the very heart of it, and then one way out. We cannot lose our way. To walk a labyrinth can be to walk a sacred path of recognising our fullest self and soul. We enter the labyrinth with our questions and we journey to centre, pausing for the time it takes until we retrace our steps as we journey back to the surface of our daily world, honouring what may emerge as insight and wisdom from this journey.

This can even be done with a finger labyrinth, a picture of a small spiral pathway that we trace with our finger. To stay on the path we must slow down. We can ponder a question or just connect mindfully to our breathing and our being. When we arrive at the centre, take a few grounding breaths and pause, then like a walking labyrinth, we can return the way we entered, perhaps responding to the simplest but often most effective question: 'Where am I right now?'

As the Chinese poet Lao Tsu writes: 'Can you stand in the water until your own mud settles?'

In Chapter 11: Additional resources and activities, you will find an example of a finger labyrinth.

Signs of imbalance or that you have not spent enough time in this season

Fear and doubt grow

You don't take time for yourself; instead of slowing down, you speed up, leading to exhaustion

It feels like you are using your energy 'reserve tank', even moving to empty

Colds come earlier than usual at the beginning of Winter, or last longer

Learning is neglected

You don't accept help easily or at all

Stillness and listening are no longer valued or they are harder to do

Critical human resources are not used well, e.g. the fresh ideas of the young or the wisdom of elders are ignored

Power is out of balance somewhere in the system

The gift of winter is Reflection, whether experienced as moments when the sense of acceptance, compassion and love meet each other within us, or as longer periods in quiet contemplation. Grace is key. It helps us face, or manage, adversity in our lives and draw on our reserves of courage to help us bear witness, and face our fears when we might otherwise be too hurried or burdened. Grace arises from within us, not from anything we can buy or acquire.

Winter intentions in the garden of life are about:

- Making use of acquired wisdom and learning throughout the year

- Drawing upon insight and quiet time to be with ourselves

- Planning what to 'crop' in Spring

- Conserving resources, going deep and being still as a cultivated practice

- Developing an inner calm that germinates creativity

- Using Winter's energy to flow inward and be with what is there with patience

- Making time to connect through poetry, walking, reading or journaling to replenish and rebalance resources

- Seeking inspiration in the mystery of the not-known and the spirit of life

The outdoor garden in Winter

The garden during Winter may look bare, but make no mistake; many things are going on beneath the surface! It is under the soil that seeds begin to germinate. The seed is fed, nurtured and protected long before it begins its journey to the soil's surface. It is traditionally a time for preparing the soil, for digging.

If it isn't frosty, bare-rooted deciduous plants and roses can be planted. If the ground isn't soggy or frozen, even established deciduous trees can be moved. Without their leaves, many trees, shrubs and hedges can be pruned and renovated.

The cold and frost change the composition of the soil by breaking it down. Plants already in the ground are resting. Early flowering ones, like snowdrops, are going to be waking up and pushing shoots through early in the calendar year. Many other plants are tending to their root systems and taking in nutrients for their arrival later in Spring. Each plant will have its own cycle, or some will have more than a single cycle in a calendar year. Each will have its phase of resting and preparing.

Thick, dry mulch or straw can protect roots from cold. Warmed soil is important for early sowing so think greenhouse or other mode to protect more tender plants with a coat of fleece to wrap them in.

The gardener does have a bit more free time now than earlier in the year. There are, though, always jobs to do. Pruning is one late Winter task. The reason for pruning is to open up the bush to more light for strong healthy growth. The harder you prune anything, the stronger will be the resulting growth, or so say some professional gardeners. So with roses you cut the very spindly shoots completely; weak ones are cut back hard and vigorous ones less so.

Some key tasks for Winter:

- Planning for winter colour in borders

- Shortening or tying long stems to protect from wind

- Taking root and basal cutting from strong perennial border plants cuttings

- Shaping young trees and staking them

- Keeping an eye on young seedlings under glass

- Sowing vegetables under cloche for early crop

It is not just in the garden that rest and preparation are key. Winter's gift for us is about nurturing and nourishing. It is a time for creating opportunities for restoration and reflection. We need to become still in order to hear the quiet voice of our most heartfelt self. This may be a time of greater connection to spirituality, our soulful self and what inspires us the most. Trust your wisdom as a guide. Each time you do, there is the invitation to bring what is not known into more conscious awareness.

Athletes and musicians know that practising, warming up and preparing make them more effective in their chosen fields. We can incorporate a 'Winter' period when we take time, and down tools to pause. Using different methods to take us easily into a reflective inward state can help, like reading a favourite poem, listening to music, taking a walk, or visiting a local place that represents a spiritual oasis for you.

Check old narratives and stories that will help you to make those happen or that could hinder you so you can deal with them, in order to give your projects the best chance of thriving.

Melissa's Winter

Melissa came to see me two winters ago. She felt she had many symptoms of stress and possibly burnout.

Melissa and her team at work had lots of simultaneous projects going on; it was hard to get going or stay focussed. She said she felt like she needed to be in five places at once. Melissa had always thrived in a go-getting environment and really liked that, yet all her work was suffering from lack of attention. Melissa discovered a pattern in the way she and her team worked. When they won a new project, the team spent time brainstorming designs and solutions until they found something just right. Then they threw themselves one hundred percent into making it happen and producing a result, while in parallel, they looked for other projects that they could pitch for... Either they had hardly enough work to keep the team going, or so much work, they worked all hours and weekends to meet the demand. Everyone was committed to the success of the company they had long dreamed of. When Melissa stepped back she could see they were rarely in balance. There was little time given to Late Summer's season of harvesting the best of what they did, in order to decide how they wanted the rest of the year to go. They had not done Autumn pruning, thinking about what might be delegated to a sub-team, or even perhaps turned away. Melissa recognised they also had no 'Winter' in their cycle. The team didn't take much time to reflect. They were astounded that they skipped this necessary process of incubation and recuperation in terms of their business and themselves. They went from seeding ideas to full-blown projects over and over.

Melissa and her team set up a monthly 'away day'. They organised a team retreat and each person identified their own pruning and pampering time. The team tried having three weeks a year when the whole office was closed. They feared this would lead to a loss of business. This turned out to be untrue. In fact, they found they worked and played much better with their 'Autumn' and 'Winter' reinstalled in the cycle of their work.

Of course, it is not just teams and organisations that can struggle in this way. We ourselves can risk burning out and running dry. No garden can survive and thrive without this part of the cycle even if it varies greatly, from urban to rural areas or from country to country. We all need time for renewal and preparation. Yet we can be afraid of stopping because there is too much to do. The more stressed we become the less we can see it. The effects of stress can make us tunnel-visioned. We can only see the objective in front of us and we lose sensitivity and awareness to everything else or conversely, we become oversensitive to everything around us because we are frazzled. The limbic system, and more specifically the amygdala, is programmed to be on red alert. The amygdala is the part of our brain that is designed to look out for potential danger. It has a hair trigger role in emotional outbursts. The term 'amygdala hijack' is coined by Daniel Goldman in his 1996 book *Emotional Intelligence: Why It Can Matter More Than IQ*.[5] Goldman uses the term to describe emotional responses that are immediate and overwhelming, and out of proportion with the actual stimulus because a much more significant emotional threat has been triggered. In that moment we lose our logical reasoning response and get caught in the emotional response of fight or flight. Adrenalin floods the body for about 20 minutes and we can experience a kind of lack of control we usually know ourselves to have. Not all hijacks are distressing. If someone tells a joke and the laughter is explosive that, too, is a limbic response. Having a collection of various ways in which we can renew our energy, and connect to our metaphorical root system, helps us be resilient. Exercise, sleep and diet are phenomenally important. Just like our garden, we need different attention in the Winter to that we need in the Summer. Learning to pay attention to our various internal cycles helps us honour ourselves and others.

Let us also note that Winter is the season of mystery. In the shadows of longer nights and shorter days, the garden of life will need to weather the hardest moments of Winter. It is a time of faith and spirit. We hold fast through the long nights and short days when clarity may have gone to ground. We need courage to hang in there, patience to wait.

It is a time to go beneath the surface and tend to the parts of us that do not get the fullness of the sun so often. It may be the parts of ourselves we are less comfortable with, or know less well. These too require attention and love and this can help us through the darkest nights. Therein lies some of our potential treasure, just like in the garden, beneath the surface of the soil...

Winter offers an opportunity for hunkering down and seeking inspiration in different ways. Sitting by the fire, and getting comfortable with the gifts of stillness, silence and solitude to be quietly with ourselves is worth experimenting with, each in our own ways. It is a season for connecting to that small voice inside us that longs to be heard, if only we stop and listen.

> ### Greenhousing point
>
> Thinking about your own patterns, what do you notice if you stand back and look over your metaphorical life garden? When have you rushed too much or not enough? Where has your energy been most lively and vigorous? Where have the parched times been? What patterns can you see emerging, over time, if any?

Cultivating Grace

The **Grit** we develop in Autumn (see Chapter 6) will partner the **Grace** we need in Winter to abide and be our own witness. We must be wise and conserve our reserves, whether they be courage, power, energy, will or the determination to use them well. Winter allows us to get up close to our ability to access the depth of who we are and glimpse into the shadows. Through reflection, we can draw on our inner wisdom and come to know and love parts of ourselves that have yet to be reclaimed. The flow at this time of the seasonal cycle is inward. Cultivating Grace is key because it allows us to be with what whatever arises with compassion and kindness, so we can 'be with' rather than 'do with'. This doesn't mean we can't make changes, but as we replenish how and who we are, we help replenish what we do. This might be through a spiritual or contemplative practice, dreams, and poetry – anything that takes us into the mystery of life itself so that we become available to the quiet voice inside us that knows so much more, if we only allow it some space.

Grace is becoming familiar with our essence as a person and walking it into the world, bearing it in our gait and in our graciousness to self and others. It is the fusion of dignity and warmth and spare movement. It is the ability to be alongside our connection with humility. For a while we quieten the fussing mind. Grace helps us to find the balance point where we can allow both the pull 'to act' and pull 'to be', to co-exist without strain, using our own presence to recognise the sweet spot for what it is and to respond from that place.

Winter practices

1. Free writing exercise – write for seven minutes on one of these topics:

   How aware are you of your personal power? How do you use it?

   What are you most deeply committed to?

   (If you have not discovered them yet, there are some tips on reflective journaling in **Chapter 11**.)

2. Develop a meditation practice

   Start with five minutes if you have never meditated before and build up from there. Aim for five of these time chunks five days per week. Find a time and a place where you won't be disturbed. Use a timer if it helps. There are some resources for beginning a mindfulness practice in **Chapter 11** to get you started if this is a new practice for you. The most important aspect is setting the time aside regularly even if that is hard to do. That alone is a space of non-doing to allow the busy-ness of the day to be put to one side briefly.

3. Take a 'media fast' for 24 hours

   No TV, computer or smartphone. Can you do it for a whole weekend? Take time to read a book, listen to music, have a massage or pamper yourself at home. Treat yourself to a retreat day.

4. Identify activities that stimulate and nurture your creativity and curiosity

   Read something different; listen to a radio station you don't usually tune into. Try a different newspaper online. See a movie that is not your first choice. Try signing up to an e-course or attending a lecture by someone whose ideas interest you. Be open to what might be restorative and nourishing.

5. Get as much sunshine as you can as the days get shorter

    Wrap up warm and get outside. Walking on fresh, cold winter days can be exhilarating. Winter sunshine helps get a dose of Vitamin D in your body. Use a light box indoors to get natural light if you are especially affected by the absence of light as the days get shorter.

6. Look for ways to exercise patience where you might not otherwise

    Where do you need to go with the flow, letting go of over-attachment to your own or others' thinking?

7. Find

    Find a book, website, or series of quotes that inspire you and give yourself some time to sit and read.

8. Reconnect

    Re-connect with your sense of spirituality in any way that enriches you.

9. Be of service to something bigger than yourself or for someone else

    Use your talents and skills to help in supporting a cause that means something to you.

10. As a way of conserving your energy, practise saying 'no' to requests

    Pay attention to how your mind and body and feelings respond to this. What old messages govern your 'yes', without thinking?

Moon phases meditation

Meditations on the moon can help us to embrace and balance our feminine (yin) and masculine (yang)-like qualities.[6] Musing about the moon can remind us of our own inherent cyclical and reflective nature so we can more gracefully accept the high and low tides of life and honour them as temporary phases.

Start by finding yourself a comfortable position in which to sit. Close your eyes and allow yourself to imagine that a new moon is about to begin its full circle journey around the Earth.

Picture a pale crescent moon beginning to appear as it is framed in the distant horizon. You can see the moon seem to grow as its colourful landscape and surroundings begin to fade as night falls. Tune into the gentle energy of the moon in this phase and absorb the yin-like quality of a relaxed, feminine energy. This is like taking a journey which invites us to wander rather than go in a direct line from A to B.

This is where we may see and experience the tangential side roads undiscovered on our way from A to B. It still gets us where we need to be, but takes us on a different kind of journey. Regardless of our gender, taking time to wander can be a joy. As you visualise the moon, feel this yin energy as it leaves you feeling nurtured and inspired, as if by a sideways smile in the sky.

Next, imagine the picture of a half moon. See how it embraces both light and dark as it perches in the heavens. For a fleeting moment, the moon's half face is full of light and yet we can just about see the edges of the darker side if we try. Now, you can see a big, bright full moon in a dark, inky night sky. You are completely surrounded by a velvety heaven, speckled with twinkling stars. It is like a temporary spotlight on the world. The moon does not emit its own source of light but it has the ability to reflect the sun's rays. What would it be like if you are the full moon, reflecting the light that comes from your unique source of who you are? Feel yourself shining bright, a powerful light going in all directions containing both yin and yang energy.

Lastly, visualise the waning moon as it begins to vanish back into the depth of the dark sky. Once again there will be the opportunity for a fresh new start as the ebb and flow of the moon's cycle repeats its journey.

Trust in your own cycles that contain both the light and the dark, knowing that no matter how you appear to those around you, you are always a full, rounded integral part of the wonderful and mysterious universe. Take a final moment to connect inside to what this means for you.

The next time you look up into the night sky and see the moon waxing or waning, give yourself a moment to remind yourself of its qualities in yourself and in others.

A story for Winter: Demeter and Persephone

From ancient times, people have used stories to explain and to talk about the cycle of the seasons. The story of Demeter and Persephone is one of the most well-known Greek myths.

Demeter was a goddess who stood for the abundance of the earth. She was loved by all people for her gifts of fertile soil and gentle mild weather to grow their crops. Unlike a number of the other gods who spent their time in lofty Olympus, Demeter was right at home in the fields at harvest time.

Persephone was Demeter's only child and she too was beloved by all. She was kind and caring with a friendly warmth about her. She brought light and happiness wherever she went.

Persephone and her mother were very close and they loved spending time together. Demeter saw her child grow into a radiant young woman. This was about to change.

One day, Persephone had been out collecting flowers in the countryside to bring home for her mother. Unbeknown to her, Hades, the god of the Underworld, was spying on her. He had fallen deeply in love with her and wanted to make her his wife. He knew that Demeter would never agree to let her dear child go down to the gloomy world of the dead. Hades decided to visit Zeus, Olympian god of the sky and the thunder, king of all other gods and men, who agreed to Hades' plan to abduct Persephone and take her back to his realm.

As Persephone wandered through the grass and fields she could sense little birds beginning to twitter anxiously. The sky turned dark. There was a deep rumble that shook the very air. The ground began to shudder and all of a sudden a great chasm appeared in the earth before her. Horrified, she could see Hades in his black and gold horse-drawn chariot rise up. He scooped up the shocked young woman, whose flowers spilled dead from her hand, and put her into the chariot.

He turned his chariot around and disappeared back into the ground. No matter how much Persephone cried for help, the deeper and deeper they plunged into the dark world beneath the ground.

Hades had always had a sad and lonely life. He was enchanted by fair Persephone. No matter how much he pleaded for her to stay and be his wife, the more she cried. She stopped eating and did not respond to any appeal from Hades and said she would not marry him.

Demeter meanwhile was sick with grief. Her daughter had disappeared. She roamed the countryside searching far and wide with no sign of her. From anger came her sadness and despair and as a consequence the earth was sad along with her. The crops began to fail, the land became barren, and a thick cold fog crept over the earth.

In her desperate cry for help, the Sun god, Helios, heard her and took pity on her. He told her the truth about what had happened as he had seen it in his daily journey across the sky.

Demeter's fury knew no restraints. It was a terrible and savage, vengeful rage that ignited in her heart. She called all the gods to bear witnesses to her words: 'Never again will there be a fruitful crop until I once again see my daughter'. This worried Zeus very much because if the people were hungry and began to starve they would stop worshipping him. He called Hermes, his messenger, to go to Hades and bring Persephone back.

By this time Persephone had learned more about the underground realm and felt sorry for Hades. With his patience and sincerity she had begun to enjoy his company. Hades, too, could tell that Persephone was of two minds.

Persephone had, up to this point, refused food, knowing that once you eat of the table of Hades you can never leave. She decided to accept a few pomegranate seeds. Just six.

Hermes saw this and thought that she was now committed to stay. He used his persuasive powers to negotiate. She had eaten of her own free will so she had to be in the Underworld, but Demeter was also calling her back. So the decision was made that Persephone would return home for six months, beginning in Spring. In so doing, Demeter agreed to make sure flowers blossomed in the fields and meadows to welcome her daughter home. After harvest in the Autumn when the leaves fell and the crops finished, her daughter would willingly return to Hades, her husband, as queen of the Underworld for six months, one for every seed she had eaten. And every year onward forever after, this cycle would repeat each Spring.

Postcard from the Winter Hedgerow

Preparing for your weekly seasonal walks

1. First start by finding a place to sit or be at rest.

Take a few moments to get a sense of where you are. Become aware of where you are sitting or standing. Your feet should be flat on the ground, with your body balanced evenly between both feet. Shoulders are relaxed back and down and your spine erect but not rigid. Have your knees ever so slightly bent. If you are sitting, have both feet flat on the ground, arms relaxed, perhaps in your lap. You may wish to drop your gaze down to the ground to remove any distractions or close your eyes if it feels comfortable for you to do so where you are.

Bring your attention to your breath and notice where you feel your in and out breathing most distinctly. It could be your abdomen, your chest, or the sensation of cool air flowing in and out of your nostrils. Follow the pace of your breath in and out without changing anything, just following it as it flows naturally for a few moments, perhaps a minute or two. Allow your body to release any tension.

When you are centred in yourself, reconnect with your body as it sits or stands where it is. Feel the holding solidity of the ground beneath your feet or the firmness of the chair or bench where you sit.

2. Consider your intention for your walk today.

You might choose a word or a quality or use one of the questions below as a walking prompt. If you do then let the question rest lightly as you walk, allowing whatever arrives in your head and heart to be. You can use the same questions over many weeks or choose a different one. You may notice different experiences presenting.

3. Use all of your senses.

When you are ready, begin your walk by holding openness to the qualities of the season in mind. Allow yourself to tune into what you can see, hear and sense on your walk – almost perhaps as if you were seeing it for the first time.

Over the next weeks and months of the season, pay close attention to newness as you walk, increasing your range of noticing what is new and fresh in you or in Nature, the parks and gardens around you as the season shifts day by day and week by week.

4. Give yourself a few uninterrupted moments to really look at something from every angle.

See it as if you had never seen one of its kind before in your life. Sniff it, touch it gently. Turn it over if you can. Close your eyes for a moment with it resting in your hand or on your finger. Think about its journey up to now and how it may have come into existence. Take in the nuance of its shade or colour, texture, line, and position.

5. Capture the essence at the finish for your Season's diary.

Use your *Postcard from the Hedgerow* to capture some words or a quick sketch, whatever suits you, that most helpfully summarises your walk. These cards, as the weeks go by, will be part of your weekly bite-size journaling. They capture a moment in time and are added to your collection as you travel through the year. Of course you may also want to write more but if you are new to journal writing this is a wonderful place to start because the space does not demand so much and they are very easy to carry with you anywhere.

Winter walks

Begin with a few moments to ground yourself and follow your breath mindfully. Winter walks can be very satisfying and invigorating. The secret is to wrap up warm and take your journal and maybe a camera with you to capture key words and images. After each weekly walk pick two or three key points and capture them on your postcard. These will be your seeds for next year.

Here are some questions to think through as you take your walks over the course of the season. To support your intentions put the weekly walk dates in your diary for the whole season so that they are part of your schedule.

Questions to ponder on your Winter walks:

1. What have you noticed over the last 12 months that has helped you be courageous in the face of challenging situations, small or large?

2. In the garden we cover the most fragile plants with fleece. The greenhouse protects the young and less hardy. How do you protect your most vulnerable self?

3. If you could create or bring into life your most desired dream, what would it be and what might a first step towards it be like?

4. As you walk through Nature in this season what would you like to learn about or find out more about if you could explore any topic in the world?

5. On your walk, find one aspect of Nature around you that encapsulates how you feel, what the Winter means for you, and take a photo of it. Write about in your journal.

"Turn away from your phones, the computers and the rush,
And find the quiet stillness inside you, which is always there
And which is your own secret garden,
Your private oasis,
Your beautiful sanctuary,
And your wise guide as you go back into the world"

Elaine Patterson, *The Gift Inside Us All*

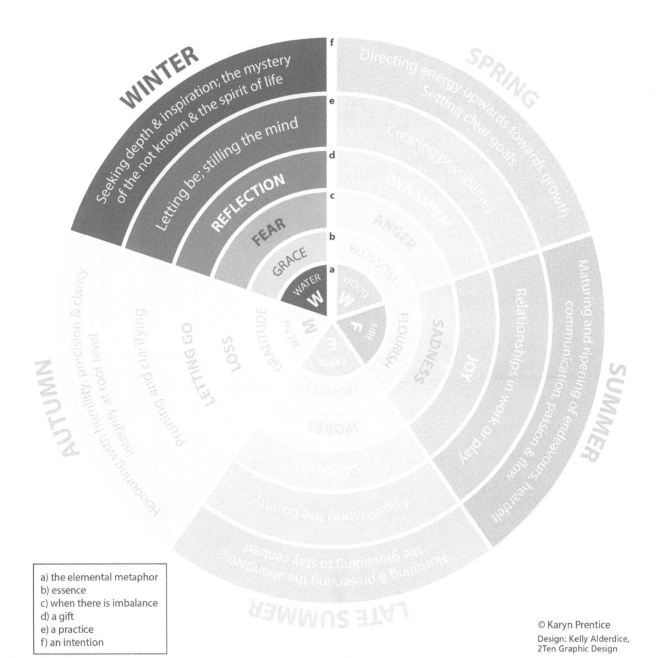

WINTER

Seeking depth & inspiration; the mystery of the not known & the spirit of life

Letting be; stilling the mind

REFLECTION

FEAR

GRACE

WATER

SPRING

Directing energy upwards towards growth

Setting clear goals

Creating possibilities

DYNAMISM

ANGER

BLOSSOM

WOOD

SUMMER

Maturing and ripening of endeavours; heartfelt communication, passion & flow

Relationships in work or play

JOY

SADNESS

FLOURISH

FIRE

LATE SUMMER

Nurturing & preserving the abundance; the grounding to stay centred

Appreciating the bounty

HUMOUR

WORRY

HARVEST

EARTH

AUTUMN

Honouring with humility precision & clarity

Integrity at root level

Pruning and clarifying

LETTING GO

LOSS

GRATITUDE

METAL

a) the elemental metaphor
b) essence
c) when there is imbalance
d) a gift
e) a practice
f) an intention

CHAPTER 3
spring

It never ceases to thrill me when I spot the first tight buds of new growth on the trees and bushes I pass on my regular morning walk, heralding the arrival of Spring. The light has begun to arrive earlier in the day and lasts a little longer at the end of the day. As if shucking off the long coat of Winter slumber, plants are daring to get going. The pace of life quickens. The sap is rising in the trees. Day by day and week by week new signs of green shoots are appearing. On the Winter-Spring cusp, England hosts one of the greatest shows I know: Spring arriving in wave after wave of splendid flowers and a riot of colours.

It is like a continuous parade of divas, each arriving on a sunlit stage, each version of natural beauty taking the spotlight, being her best: from the early appearance of snowdrops on the Winter-Spring cusp, to daffodils, which in turn give way to tulips and hyacinths, laburnum and apple blossom, to wisteria, and irises, to name only a few.

A favourite place for me at this time of year is Govern, in Normandy, not far from Paris, at the gardens Claude Monet created in 1916, where he lived for 43 years. Govern is a tiny hamlet near the town of Vernon. It is not only the home of his famous paintings of the wisteria-covered Japanese bridge, and water lilies from this wonderful garden, but many other unbelievable spring displays. In May, Govern has a spectacular display of dozens of varieties of iris in the most luscious colours grown in abundance, row upon row.

For the Spring gardener it is perhaps the most intensely busy time as everything starts to move upwards and outwards. It is time to prepare the soil, clear away and make space, set seed trays and tend to tender young plants too fragile to leave the protective greenhouse space, plant out new plants and then pamper, tend, nourish and water.

When you think of Spring, think of the hibernating bear waking up to the sharp light of early Spring. She has given birth in her burrow. She is hungry and eager to find food. The rush of refreshed earth and the quickening of the energy rising up brings with it the new life created in Winter. In this sense, timing is as critical as patience.

Plants move towards the light. They are programmed to do the only thing they are meant to do: grow, and in some cases unaided by humankind but certainly in partnership with insects, birds and the elements; to reproduce themselves. The momentum is upward from our roots.

Getting there may be straightforward but can be circuitous or delayed. I remember finding an abandoned pot behind our greenhouse that had been accidently covered by several other pots so no light or water reached it for some months. When it was uncovered there was a strong live shoot sticking up over the edge of the pot. We named the plant 'ballsy blue' because it was such a determined little thing which, no thanks at all to us, was determined to make its way into the world and be born.

Qualities associated with Spring

Funnelling energy into creativity and action

Emergence

Structure, direction, motivation

Releasing power developed underground during Winter

Vision and forward thinking

Holding the vision, planting seeds and fostering new beginnings

Initiating action

Creating relationships and partnerships

Clarifying roles, priorities, timelines

Supporting new growth

Being effectively organised

Recognising that timing is as critical as patience

Blossoming

Signs of imbalance or when you have not spent enough time in this season

Anger arises, as does impatience and frustration

False starts pepper attempts to get going on a project

Indecision or poor planning is in evidence

New ideas are not given a chance to be explored and die quickly

Nurture is low on the agenda

You focus on the past or what was rather than what is and what could begin

Too scattered, poor planning

Big shifts in emotions, pushing for outcomes rather than simply watching for growth

Trying to control too many things

Overambitious, spreading self too thin

Not being flexible, too rigid

Structure and direction

Potential to create

Releasing inner power

Initiating action

New beginnings

Growth upwards

The gift of creativity

If the gift of Spring is creativity in all its glorious forms, then the practice of looking for and looking after fresh possibilities is a Spring practice.

Following a reflective Winter, seemingly overnight new green shoots of Spring begin to appear. In the garden of life Spring invites us to bring fresh eyes to see the new, the different, and the extraordinary in the ordinary in and around us. It is a time of rebirth as well as a space for the brand new. The practice of bringing a sense of curiosity and aliveness to our observation skills is an important part of creativity.

Looking after new possibilities and projects so they have a chance to flourish means balancing our strategies for protecting the new in order to sustain it and ourselves into full growth over the season and into the Summer and Late Summer ahead, with the drive towards over-doing, because everything is exciting.

Creativity is not purely the domain and territory of artists, musicians and painters. As the creative gardener of your own life, recognising and connecting to a greater source of the creativity in you is like discovering treasure. Questions such as: 'What if...?', 'How about...?', 'I wonder if...?', are 'go to' questions that can open the doors and windows in our creative hearts and minds. We need both our analytic mind to set goals and devise plans, and we need our willingness to play with ideas, alone and with others, to help take the green shoots of new thinking forward.

Awakening is key

Spring is a time for experimentation, daring and courage to push ourselves to new learning. In Spring, awakening is key. This sense of awakening can gather momentum, as in the garden, when everything begins to take off. Here we are looking at enjoying and exploring what is, awakening to our own senses and, at the same time, being careful to look after balancing our energy, as we can be pulled between the polarity of going for everything with maximum energy and delight, our Winter patience giving way to surging forward, and keeping an eye on the big picture and what is required for resilience for the long game.

Spring intentions in the garden of life

Directing energy upwards and towards growth

Setting clear goals

Cultivating a mindset of hope over despair

Taking vision into action planning

Initiating projects and creating partnerships

Developing vigilance for balance and protecting fledgling
ideas and projects

Recognising the regular and ongoing daily and weekly tasks
required to maintain a good life garden

Staying on course to reach for the stars

Remaining resilient and robust for the whole growing season

Now try this:

Get some paper and pens and think about the current design of your life garden. This is a time to think about your vision of what is important and make new choices about what you want, your well-being, and sense of what is flourishing for you this year. What do you really like in the garden that is already there? What new ideas do you want to plan for that will, over the coming months, begin to blossom? In some cases, the blossoming may not be the final product but a stage in the growth of something longer term.

Use the garden for life plan (see Chapter 8), if you have not done so already. Take the time to gather as many ideas about what to put in your garden, and what to take out. It is also a time to network. Working with others to share ideas and explore new possibilities, contacts and resources for the benefit of all provides an opportunity to build fresh alliances and commitments for new projects.

Spring and the element of wood

In Chinese medicine the element that is related to Spring is wood. Wood has the ability to grow both upwards and downwards at the same time. As humans, when we look after mind, body and spirit in a way that helps us be aligned in our values, we are growing down into the root system of our values and beliefs like good roots in soil and when we are clear in what we want, we can grow upwards and outwards to new beginnings based upon what we have learned. Many plants produce new growth on the wood from the year before.

In terms of climate, Spring is also linked to wind. In nature, wind helps to spread seeds but too much strong wind can also challenge and break plants.

Spring is also about seeding more than one needs in order to see what will emerge into potential new plants and which will not, then selecting which tender shoots to nurture to maturity later in the cycle. Researching and gathering information is a good way to help decide what might seed well. Be creative in observing and curious to follow ideas but without too much attachment at this stage. Wood is also about holding the direction, navigating obstacles, going with the flow, making distinctions, and being clear in perception.

Cultivating a growth mindset

Abraham Maslow, a pioneer in the field of humanistic psychology, is often attributed with this impactful quote: 'In any given moment, you will either step forward into growth or you step back into safety. Growth must be chosen again and again; fear must be overcome again and again.'[7] One day the ground is smooth earth and the next day there is a small curlicue of a tiny leafed head that grows, perhaps even next to a bit of leftover snow. Barely there, yet within record time it shows itself to be the result of the bulb planted last October. New parts from seed ideas and plans begin to proliferate by the day. How we shape our own lives for new growth to freshen, enhance and esteem our own lives varies as much from person to person as garden to garden. And often it is one step at a time, gathering our courage to push out a little further with something that is new to us, different from what we usually do or even way outside of our comfort zone. Little by little, we face our fears in order to grow.

Michael Jordan, the international basketball star, testifies to his relationship to failure. 'I've missed more than 9000 shots in my career; I've lost almost 300 games. Twenty-six times I've been trusted to take the game winning shot and missed. I've failed over and over again in my life. And that's why I succeed.'[8] We have to stay curious and learn from what doesn't work so we can keep on learning. If we stop, our curiosity fades away. We lose our Spring.

Try this exercise: knowing your root system

Take some paper and draw a picture of a tree – any kind of tree will do. The tree is going to be standing for you. Leave enough room at the bottom of the paper for your root system and enough at the top for the tree's canopy of leaves and branches. The trunk represents the core values that are intrinsic to who you are. So you might have one for integrity, or family, or for any value that is strong, important and intrinsic to you. If you are not sure what kinds of things this could be then see the exercise in the back of this book for more inspiration (Chapter 11: Additional resources and activities).

Also here include the qualities and capacities as a human being that make you who you are. Like trees in the Northern Hemisphere that have a resting period, the rings that form, if you looked at a tree slide, would tell you its age. This is not the case for all trees, everywhere. Trees that grow in places like Central America have no dormant period. They grow all year round and have no rings, so telling the age of a tree can be more difficult.

In the root system allow a root line for:

- lessons learned from successes

- lessons learned from the knocks in life

- your ancestry and stories passed down through generations

- your primary family, parents or care-givers when you were a child

- stories or scripts that have influenced the way you see life

- your education

- rules that guide you about how to be okay in the world

The branches of the tree represent the skills and strengths you have developed through jobs, roles you hold at home, in the community or you have grown over time and effort. They may be things people say about you, that you are good at, or that they like and admire and appreciate in you. They may be the strengths that you have worked hard to acquire for yourself or ones that you have had for a long time and come naturally to you.

Add as many as feel right for you. This is just a snapshot of now. Your tree will continue to grow all of your life. Be creative with your tree. For instance, you may have branches for different jobs, or for specific projects, or tasks, or achievements. You might add a branch for an activity you spent time on and learned a lot from. Add anything else you think is important for your tree.

Qualities   Skills

Values   Capabilities

Influences

Reflection point:

- What kind of a tree is it?

- Does your tree have blossom, fruit or berries?

- Is your tree leafy or bare, tall, short, and what kind of tree is it?

- Is it an evergreen or does it lose its foliage in autumn?

- Is it tall, broad, old or young?

- What else?

Greenhousing point

Take some time to journal about your tree. One method that might be interesting to try is to write from the first person perspective, speaking as your tree. Give yourself some time to let your imagination take you where you need to go. Don't edit or stop writing, just put down the experience of your tree as it is and what Spring feels like from the perspective of your tree.

Greenhousing point

How invested are you in seeding for your own future, whatever that may mean?

What do you want to plant and what would you hope to crop in Late Summer or Autumn?

What can you accommodate now and over time?

What do you need to do now to allow new thoughts, ideas, and projects to show themselves?

The outdoor garden in Spring

The gardener is constantly engaged in Spring with a multitude of tasks. Not that a gardener ever stops tending the garden, whatever the season, but now the sap begins to rise. The soil is slowly warming up, there is so much calling for attention. Early Spring will see the planning of Autumn and the germination of Winter show up in decisions about what to plant. This is a time to plant seeds into trays before transferring them at the appropriate moment to pots and the ground. Bulbs that have completed their cycle are ready to emerge from the ground in late Spring. Dead heading of spent blooms and from last year's herbaceous plants encourages flourishing. Taking cuttings of strong plants will generate the 'offspring' of mature plants.

Gardeners usually have a wealth of seed packets they have accumulated. They may have over-wintered cuttings from successful parent plants or grandparent plants. They swap seeds and cuttings with other gardeners to bring newness and fresh colour into the garden.

The gardener is also engaged in less sexy, but just as vital, activities like lawn care, mowing and weeding. A gardener only has to turn their back for a short time and weeds appear unbidden, vigorous, and relentlessly everywhere. It's also good to give the soil a light forking over to keep it aerated.

Some key tasks for Spring:

- Growing plants from seeds and sowing young plants

- Sowing hardy annuals, bedding plants and climbers

- Planting perennial borders and summer bedding at the end of May

- Pinching off spent bulb heads to encourage further flowering

- Feeding plants to stimulate growth

- Taking soft cuttings of garden shrubs

- Looking after the lawn and mowing, weeding and collecting compost

"Possibility is the secret heart of creativity"

John O'Donohue

Spring practices

What new opportunities are presenting in your life? What is just under the surface waiting for your curiosity to find it? Where does hope sit in your repertoire of growth?

1. Take some time to take stock and spring clean your thinking. How do you assess and choose new beginnings and also stay grounded? You can't choose them all. Judicious pricking out and potting is important to give the strongest ideas a chance to grow even stronger. Consider how you will balance your energies.

2. Imagine what you would like to plant in your life's garden. What would it be? What would your design help you harvest later on in the year that will matter to you? What do you need in order to stay supple along the way? What skills do you need to cultivate?

3. Create some 'tea cup' goals. Tea cup goals are small, perfectly formed goals that give us a sense of pleasure to achieve them, partly because they don't take too long to carry out, so success quickly follows intention. With a minimum of effort we get a maximum result – like a beautifully made cup of tea. It quenches the thirst, whatever the thirst is. For example, letting yourself take that long, slow bath instead of a quick shower, getting the Indian head massage that has been on your wish list for months, if not longer. Picking up the phone and calling someone you love...

   Here are the criteria for a tea cup goal:

   ✓ It can be completed in one to three days and in no more than five steps or moves.

   ✓ It has a specific action as the outcome that is within your power to accomplish, e.g. look up something on the internet, get out for a walk, call someone, make some notes, go and do something a short radius from your home that you can plan into the day.

   ✓ You have enough autonomy and control to make it happen without anyone else's permission or approval.

   ✓ You can imagine yourself feeling pleased when you have completed it.

Ask yourself what plan can be accomplished in no more than five steps. A tea cup goal can comprise part of a bigger goal. The rules still apply. No more than five steps or moves and no more than 72 hours to complete it. Sometimes people settle on too big a task at a time and run out of motivation part way through, or it is a good task but out of sequence with all the other necessary things to accomplish the main goal. Tea cup goals are small enough to trigger a sense of accomplishment, which is often just what we need.

4. Managing strong feelings is part of the Spring surge. Like sap rising in the trees, Spring can cause a flare up of energy that can present itself as creativity, even anger. When the energy rises it can also flare when frustration meets an obstacle. Anger in itself can be a powerhouse for moving ahead with strongly felt goals. It can spur us on through the injustices in the world to fight for causes that are congruent with our own belief system. Whether you direct your anger into creativity, or allow it to blow over, finding a way to explore this vulnerability safely in constructive, helpful and potentially positive ways is a challenge. Good Spring practice is to find creative challenges for strong feelings. If you feel you need to let off steam, how can your anger be challenged effectively for you and for others around you?

5. Keep a senses diary. The more we journal about our senses the more we tune into them. Keeping a senses diary means to be in connection with your senses and experiences. We can better savour what we can really participate in and this can help us tune into what we feel. Try making a daily entry in your journal, one for each of the five senses, over a week and see what they evoke for you.

6. Plant something! Even if space is a real consideration, find a pot or a container that you can manage if you don't have garden space. A window sill of herbs, a small pot that can be home to some seed or plant that you can tend and watch grow close to hand is a great Spring practice. If you have a garden to play in then this is the time to be choosing what to grow and starting off some seed trays. Find other gardeners and offer to do a 'seed swap' so you can share a wider range of growing possibilities.

7. Plant a tree for someone else or as part of a Spring volunteer force for an outdoor organisation like The National Trust, English Heritage or the Wildlife Trust in your local area.

Reflecting on the word 'Spring'

Collect together four pictures of different ways to experience the word 'Spring'. Here are some headings that might appeal: *Leap, spring blossom, bounce, coiled spring, spring clean, spring of water.*

You might choose a picture of your own garden, a park, or countryside in blossom, for instance. You might pick pictures of a waterfall or a flowing brook or river or a person springing up into the air. Almost anything that you feel stands for Spring will do.

Find a quiet space where you won't be bothered for a half hour and lay out the four images.

We are going to take some time to reflect on the word 'Spring', and on how its different meanings show up in our daily lives. Have your journal by your side to capture what seems important to you, either as you go along or after the whole exercise.

Bounce

When we are out walking, sometimes we have to leap over a ditch or up a bank. Or at work, we have to raise energy in a group brainstorming session and we sometimes describe this as 'bouncing ideas off each other'. We may 'bounce' from one task to another. It is a jump of energy and has a different feel from the word 'leap' which could conjure a jump from the known to the unknown. Take three minutes to contemplate what 'bounce' means to you. Allow your imagination to wander. You can use your phone as a timer to let you know when to come back to the here and now. When you look at your chosen pictures is there any connection to either 'bounce' or 'leap'?

Spring blossom

Spring is a season that stands for new life and renewal bursting out everywhere. Perhaps there are some still familiar sights from the previous season. Things look fresher. There is colour, bird song and more light. What does your picture tell you about what is ready to flower in you? Take three minutes to reflect on this.

Spring clean

Spring shows up for us in the familiar as well as the new. Are there things that you need to reacquaint yourself with, get rid of or recycle?

In taking stock in our life garden we may find we have to do some Spring cleaning in ourselves so that we can refresh and prepare ourselves for new growth.

Take three minutes to sit quietly and reflect on what needs a good clear out in your garden so that you have space to plant something new. Where will you make the space for new growth? What must now be cleared away so that you can flourish?

Coiled spring

This kind of Spring is resilient. It returns to its original shape when pulled or contracted. In us this Spring might be thought of as the power greater than our everyday self. In whatever way we might experience this, it is a sense of resilience, or spirituality or even our immense potential to be all we can be or experience more than we think we can. It might be the part of us that we call upon in emergencies or a part that utterly surprises us when hearing some beautiful music and we are touched to our very core.

Take three minutes to sit quietly with the notion of being more than your everyday self and how that might resonate with you. What motivates you when you have had to go the extra mile or three?

Spring of water

This Spring might be bursting out of the rocks, or from the ground beneath us and flows through the land freshening and re-vitalising as it goes. Perhaps it is the melting of mountain snow becoming a waterfall. Even its sound is refreshing when we are hot and dry. It provides water to drink and to wash in. The source has beckoned humankind for all time. Take three minutes to consider all the ways you resource yourself, or could do so that you stay refreshed and vital.

Spring meditation

Ostara is the Goddess of Spring and the Dawn. The worship of this goddess, like many goddesses in ancient myth, has its roots in ancient Pagan Teutonic and Saxon cultures. Some contemporary pagans still have rituals that honour her at Spring Equinox time. It is said that the festival of Easter was named for Ostara and from this stem the symbols of Easter eggs, bunnies, coloured eggs and springtime celebrations.

For this meditation find a comfortable, safe, and quiet place. Close your eyes. Relax and centre yourself by taking deep slow breaths.

Imagine that you are in a hilly countryside. It is just before sunrise in early Spring. Perhaps there is frost or even snow still visible on the ground. You face the east and watch the sun as it begins to rise, throwing its rising light over the land around you. Get a sense of yourself in this opening up of the day.

Now, as the sun rises you have a sense of a fresh new day coming up from the earth, full of possibility. You may sense the goddess herself appearing on the land, or it may take the form of an animal, plant or simply a colour or sound. Connect to what the Spring really means for you, right now in this moment, as a symbol of hope and renewal. As you sit with what arises, try to sense what the nature of fresh beginnings means for you in your life.

As you get a sense of this wise presence coming closer you see that she is carrying a golden basket filled with coloured eggs. You see that with each step the land around her bursts into new life. New grasses sprout from the ground. Herbs flourish. Trees are putting out new leaves in beautiful shades of green.

You greet her and this Spring that calls out to you, and you feel personally welcomed by Spring itself. The goddess or whoever has embodied this essence of Spring for you holds the golden basket toward you and invites you to choose one of the eggs in it as a gift of Spring. You notice that each egg has a different colour. Some are jewelled and some simple. There is a wonderful choice. You feel yourself more drawn to one of the eggs than the others and choose it. Hold the egg that you have selected in both of your hands.

First focus on its colour and reflect on what that colour means to you. Then you are invited to think about what would help you plant and tend your garden the most this Spring. Take a few moments in silence as you pay attention to whatever words, images, somatic responses and/or other forms of message emerge.

You are now invited to take this specially chosen egg with its sacred power of new growth into yourself. Hold it to your heart and as you do this, absorb the qualities it brings to you. As you do so, notice how this gift impacts on you. Rest with this for a few moments. Perhaps you have an upsurge in energy, or a greater vitality. Be fully present with this experience.

Prepare to retune to where you began this meditation. Bid goodbye to your wise guide or essence with the knowledge that what they bring to you will remain yours as you journey through the season. As you walk back to where you began, take in the landscape all around you, take a deep breath and gently open your eyes. Slowly stand up and stretch, and come back to the here and now. Take a few moments now and note down your experiences. Let the vitality of Spring renewal continue to be with you as you go about your daily life.

YES

This morning I am saying yes.
Perhaps success is simply embracing
This moment, these sounds, this full heart.
If this is what life most asks of us,
Then I am full.

I am saying yes to wake up today,
To seeing early morning light and quiet streets.
Yes to the men who seem
To have slept on the beach,
Now joining in the café
Sharing coffee and the local paper,
Greeting one another in familiar tones,

Yes to the people sitting alone

With coffee and a morning muffin
Starting their days,
And to the bright-eyed woman
Making coffee with friendly greetings.

Yes to the little girl sitting on mom's lap,
Hands mingled, smiling.
Yes to the look of concerned,
Furrowed brows over mom's eyes
Hidden by dark glasses.
Her day is starting just as it is.
And yes to the old songs on the radio
Played in this beach side place for decades.

Yes to my day already in motion
And to each person I meet.
Yes to life, to our common goal of living.
You, dear friend
Where is your YES today?

Sam Magill from *Fully Human*

Spring tips

SPRING TIP 1 Don't throw all your seeds into one hole.

SPRING TIP 2 Be aware of your patterns.

SPRING TIP 3 Use your greenhouse to nurture tender ideas until they are ready to take out into the world. Tend.

SPRING TIP 4 As you set a plan into action be aware of small changes taking place.

SPRING TIP 5 Sometimes you plant one thing and something else comes up!

If nothing comes up ask:

- *Do I really want this and why?*

- *What will it be like for me if this comes up? If it doesn't?*

- *What do I need to do differently?*

SPRING TIP 6 Use a support system. Like runner beans, some ideas can run wild and shoot up seemingly overnight. Make sure you have the right support in place.

For you and your projects think about who can be a source of research, input, inspiration and help. Can you be a support for someone else?

- *People who know you and what you have to offer*

- *Don't be afraid to ask (or invite) a naïve question*

- *Be specific about the help you want – it can make all the difference*

Work back chart

Planning ahead is a good Spring activity. A 'work back chart' is one very simple tool for thinking out the steps of a project you are interested in, or a goal you want to achieve.

To make one you only need a stack of Post-it notes and a large, wide blank space, like a wall, as a temporary canvas for sticking the notes to while you work on your plan.

Action may go forward but exploring planning by working backward helps to clarify a plan so that the right tasks are carried out in the correct order.

How many of you have had goals and dreams and despite lots of effort you petered out somewhere in the middle?

Possibly because:

1. The steps taken were a waste of time because they were the wrong steps.

2. Some of the steps may have been right but in the wrong order or at the wrong times.

3. The steps may have been right, but seemed so small and insignificant that it was too hard to see how they would get anywhere so you gave up.

In this planning method we will go from the intimidatingly large back to the reassuringly small – a tea cup goal – so we move from the feast of the whole vision to its components.

Before you can put great deeds together in reality, it helps to take them apart on paper to discover what small, steady actions and in what order, will really get you there.

Two questions are your tools:

1. Can I do this tomorrow?

If the answer is no then the next question is:

2. What would I have to get done first?

Starting from the top of the paper consider this the finished goal. Mark it on a large Post-it note. Working back from the finished goal, ask yourself what needs to have been in place in order for the goal to be achieved or completed. If there are four steps, for example, put one each on a Post-it and place it underneath.

Almost all goals begin with information-gathering; an act which requires no preparation and very little courage, yet can sweep you right up in the excitement and reality of your goal.

Build your flow chart backwards using the two questions on the previous page. Note that each of the four headings you may have identified will have a mini work back chart underneath.

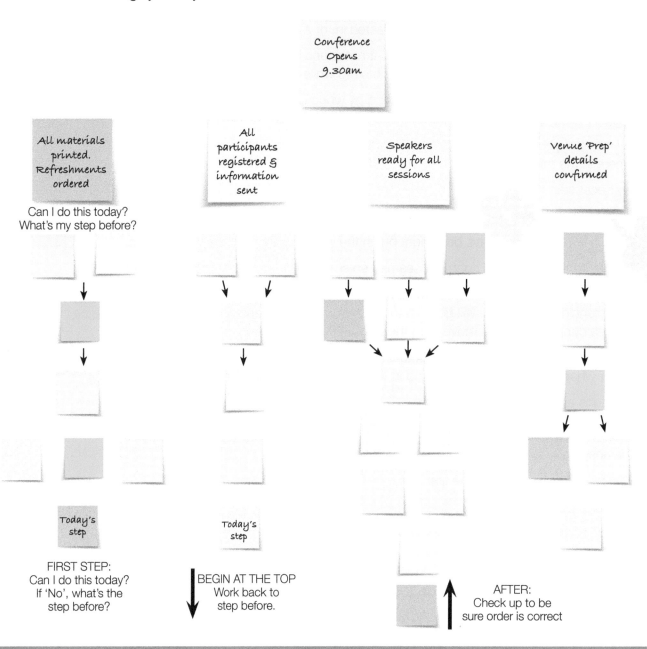

Conference Opens 9.30am

All materials printed. Refreshments ordered

Can I do this today? What's my step before?

All participants registered & information sent

Speakers ready for all sessions

Venue 'Prep' details confirmed

Today's step

Today's step

FIRST STEP:
Can I do this today?
If 'No', what's the step before?

BEGIN AT THE TOP
Work back to step before.

AFTER:
Check up to be sure order is correct

Postcard from the Spring Hedgerow

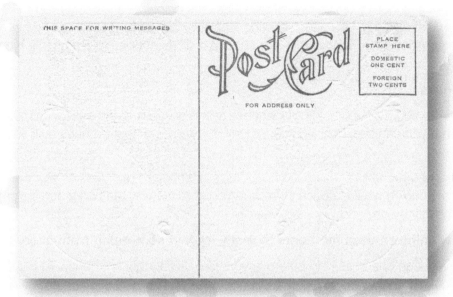

Preparing for your weekly seasonal walks

1. First start by finding a place to sit or be at rest.

Take a few moments to get a sense of where you are. Become aware of where you are sitting or standing. Your feet should be flat on the ground, with your body balanced evenly between both feet. Shoulders are relaxed back and down and your spine erect but not rigid. Have your knees ever so slightly bent. If you are sitting have both feet flat on the ground, arms relaxed, perhaps in your lap. You may wish to drop your gaze down to the ground to remove any distractions or close your eyes if it feels comfortable for you to do so where you are.

Bring your attention to your breath and notice where you feel your in and out breathing most distinctly. It could be your abdomen, your chest, or the sensation of cool air flowing in and out of your nostrils. Follow the pace of your breath in and out without changing anything, just following it as it flows naturally for a few moments, perhaps a minute or two. Allow your body to release any tension.

When you are centred in yourself, reconnect with your body as it sits or stands where it is. Feel the holding solidness of the ground beneath your feet or the firmness of the chair or bench where you sit.

2. Consider your intention for your walk today.

You might choose a word or a quality or use one of the questions below as a walking prompt. If you do then let the question rest lightly as you walk, allowing whatever arrives in your head and heart to be. You can use the same questions over many weeks or choose a different one. You may notice different experiences presenting.

3. Use all of your senses.

When you are ready, begin your walk by holding openness to the qualities of the season in mind. Allow yourself to tune into what you can see, hear and sense on your walk – almost perhaps as if you were seeing it for the first time.

Over the next weeks and months of the season pay close attention to newness as you walk, increasing your range of noticing what is new and fresh in you or in Nature, the parks and gardens around you as the season shifts day by day and week by week.

4. Give yourself a few uninterrupted moments to really look at something from every angle.

See it as if you had never seen one of its kind before in your life. Sniff it, touch it gently. Turn it over if you can. Close your eyes for a moment with it resting in your hand or on your finger. Think about its journey up to now and how it may have come into existence. Take in the nuance of its shade or colour, texture, line, and position.

5. Capture the essence at the finish for your Season's diary.

Use your *Postcard from the Hedgerow* to capture some words or a quick sketch, whatever suits you, that most helpfully summarises your walk. These cards, as the weeks go by, will be part of your weekly bite-size journaling. They capture a moment in time and are added to your collection as you travel through the year. Of course you may also want to write more but if you are new to journal writing this is a wonderful place to start because the space does not demand so much and they are very easy to carry with you anywhere.

Questions to ponder on your Spring walks

Use one or a combination on your weekly walks, or create your own.
- What would you like to see blossom?
- What tender shoots of thinking or planning are around for you?
- How might you need to be bold, strong and energised in supporting the growth of a new plan or idea?
- Where are you flexible and resilient?
- Where in a situation in your work or life do you want to take a stand, hold your ground?
- How are you being creative?

SPRING

WINTER

Seeking depth & inspiration; the mystery of the not known & the spirit of life

Letting be; stilling the mind

REFLECTION

GRACE

SPRING

f — Directing energy upwards towards growth

e — Setting clear goals

d — Creating possibilities

c — DYNAMISM

b — ANGER

BLOSSOM

WOOD

W

W

F

E

METAL

FIRE

EARTH

SUMMER

Maturing and ripening of endeavours; heartfelt communication, passion & flow

Relationships in work or play

FLOURISH

SADNESS

JOY

LATE SUMMER

Nurturing & preserving the abundance; the grounding to stay centred

Appreciating the bounty

HARVEST

WORRY

SAVOUR

GRATITUDE

AUTUMN

Honouring with humility, precision & clarity at root level

Pruning and clarifying

integrity

LETTING GO

LOSS

a) the elemental metaphor
b) essence
c) when there is imbalance
d) a gift
e) a practice
f) an intention

© Karyn Prentice
Design: Kelly Alderdice,
2Ten Graphic Design

CHAPTER 4
summer

"The goal of life is living in an agreement with nature"

Zeno 335 BC

There is a magical turning point when I know that Summer has truly arrived. It happens at the beginning and the end of the day. Even though the evening dew from the night before still lies on the grass at eight in the morning, the sun shines directly on to my patio like a spotlight, welcoming new day warmth with a different intensity to that of Spring. Away from the sunshine I might still need a sweater as I carry my breakfast out to the garden table, past the still night-damp wooden chairs just by the door. But once I have assembled all I need, I sit and savour the warmth on my body and face. I really feel the garden, and myself, fully waking up. I tilt my head back and look up at the apple tree above my head. The still small green knobs of baby apples, too many to make it to their full size in Autumn, are clustered above me, framed by vivid green leaves. This sun is just what they need to surge in size.

The dawn chorus has been in full swing for some time too. The hedge that encircles the garden is a mixture of berberis, blackberry, ivy, beech and hawthorn. From it emerges vibrant bird song, oblivious to my breakfasting presence. The hedge is like a giant apartment complex of invisible birdie residences, each singing their place in the world. It never ceases to amaze me how tiny sparrows zoom in and out like mini jet pilots unscathed by all the sharp hawthorn needles.

The other surefire Summer signal for me is at the other end of the day, when the light is beginning to soften. Along the border outside my backdoor, the sun-warmed wall and fence is home to a subtle but intoxicating perfume in the early evening. Flowers like stocks, jasmine and phlox, and aromatic herbs like rosemary and thyme release their particular aromas. This delicious fragrance signals me to take my time and not hurry past as a pungent punch of joy meets my nose. It always makes me smile.

When the sun is at its highest point in the sky and the days are longer there is a build up to the full glory of a garden, when the fruit is big and juicy, and Nature is maturing her output. It may be the gorgeous soft, velvety petals of roses, the brilliantly colourful flourishing of geraniums unabashedly loving the sun, or a Provencal field of sunflowers beginning to turn their faces to the sky as they stretch upwards. By now the grass has needed cutting at least once a week, keeping gardeners busy all the time. Weeds seem to be indestructible and reappear almost daily. Everything is whooshing upwards. Barbecues and other outdoor pleasures figure daily as people enjoy the pleasure of being outdoors.

Qualities associated with Summer

Direct communication

Sense of humour/laughter

Encouraging team work

Building relationships

Intimacy

Passion and sensuality

Celebration

Speaking from the heart

Quickness

Partnership and community

Big picture vision

Sensuality of all kinds

Understanding the other

Maintaining relationships

Maturity

Exhilarating and exciting

Revelry and celebration

Summer and the element of fire

Fires need tending. Too much flame and the blaze will be out of control; not enough and the fire will go out. A healthy degree of fire warms us and those around us. It takes only a spark to set a flame into being. In the everyday gifts of life, simple things can spark joy, compassion and vibrancy in us, with others and in nature. Our planet also calls us to love it and we can respond positively to that love by being mindful of how we use the planet's resources, as earth's guardians. Whatever else, we are in intimate relationship with the earth.

The interplay of Nature's energies is critical to life itself. When the sun is high in the sky, the days are longer and it is warmer. The element of fire brings life to creatures and warmth to the earth so we can feed ourselves. Metal, through rocks and minerals, facilitates the rain, streams, rivers, lakes and seas. Water allows plant life, forests and woods to grow. These influence the climate, which includes the sunshine, and so we come back full circle to fire. In the widest sense it is a system of controlling, holding and providing. As human beings we are like Nature, with our own cycles that support a system of controlling, holding and providing so that we may flourish and grow. How would that be true for you in your life?

In our lives fire connects us to keeping the heart open, staying in partnership with others, speaking from the heart and growing the roots of deep trust.

As humans we need to reach out. When was the last time you had a really good belly laugh? Or made others laugh? Had a hug-athon? Use touch to reassure, calm, and connect with someone compassionately.

Fire also keeps the mind sharp and gives us a glow in our eyes and belly. It helps us to stay with something, keep going and see it through. Fire energy becomes irritable or aggressive if not well channelled. We can burn the candle at both ends with energy depletion by non-stop doing. Ultimately, the aptly coined term 'burning the candle at both ends' describes the result of this imbalance, leading to overexcitement, 'up and down' moods, worry and stress. Summer is the season when you can push the boundaries out here and give it an extra burst. But balance is always the byword in the background. So go for awe, bliss, joy, passion, synergy and synchronicity. Be luscious and juicy. If not now, then when?

Cultivating glee and generosity

Summer invites us to celebrate in community and meaningful relationship with others. It is party time! Cultivating the full-fledged feeling of Summer is to embrace our gleeful, playful side. This can be a solo adventure but often is even better when it is a shared experience. It is the 'we' in relationship. Taking the dog up on the common for a brisk walk on a blue sky Summer morning is often as deeply pleasurable for the human as it is for the dog, even if in different ways. Laughter is the multicolour music of glee. In terms of this season, Summer is the culmination of the growing season for many fruits and vegetables. It is a time when plans, dreams and hopes firework their way to an apex. Enjoying it with both hands and heart open and sharing the bounty with others is to approach Summer wholeheartedly. Our capacity for connecting to glee goes hand in hand with connecting to our inner playful child who recognises the delight in discovering and exploring what is right here around us, knowing and smiling into it with an open heart.

Our generosity of spirit in these Summer moments may be to consider how we can say 'yes' to life and love in our community, team, family or in the intimacy of partnership.

The Fire of Life

Every day I bathe myself in light and write my name in stars across the sky.

Every day I am the Fire of Life, burning with the intensity of the Sun.

The Wind cannot blow away such passion, nor can Rain drown the ash of love, knowing it will burn again.

Every day I bathe myself in light and dance to the music that rivers make on their way to the sea. The Earth hears my prayers and gives my body a familiar form, feminine in nature, strong and surviving.

Every day I write my name in stars across the Universe: I am love.
The power of my flame rises with the fury of my dreams.

by Nancy Wood (1998)
from *Sacred Fire.* Courtesy of the Nancy Wood Literary Trust

Signs of imbalance or that you have not spent enough time in this season

Absence of humour or willingness to cooperate

Over-control and more *'do as I say'*, rather than co-collaborated ways forward

Feeling like you have to go it alone; a sense of isolation

Being thin skinned, taking things very personally that might not be so

Lack of vitality and aliveness

A sense of underlying chaos

Not enough or too much exhilaration

Feeling dried up

Joy is Summer's gift

Joy comes in all sizes, small or large. Children can often see what we might miss as adults in the simple pleasures, like being in cool water on a hot day, laying out on the grass looking at bugs and butterflies, imagining and inventing games in the company of others or in dreamy spaces on their own, getting lost in the moment, so absorbed in an activity that time disappears. Joy can come from being fully present in what we are doing and open to the magic of the moment. It can be big fireworks, the smell of a good barbecue or in the tender moments of intimacy shared with those we love. Summer invites us to fully participate in seeing and experiencing joy in colour, sound, taste and touch.

What is critical here is the consciousness that something really good is happening and we are in it and part of it. Joy can be fleeting, and yet often not far away. So the invitation is also to be more aware and look out for the gift. Sometimes hidden in the most seemingly ordinary activities, deep joy can reside, like looking up and catching a beautiful sunset.

Flourish

The key to Summer is to flourish. What the garden of our life needs from us to create the conditions for a flourishing life may have been germinated over Winter in our reaching down into our sense of who we are, and the meaning we want to create in our life. In Spring, plans and projects to create the conditions for flourishing may have been set in motion. Now, in Summer, we can really step into the well-being we have created and enjoy it. What it means to be flourishing will change from person to person. When we flourish, we gain more vitality and resilience. In the seasonal sense, Summer's flourish accentuates what is full, ripe, and bursting with life. The gift is to live with it in the moment. For more resources for flourishing see Chapter 11.

Summer intentions in the garden of life are about:

Looking for ways to celebrate what is good

Bringing a light touch and high energy

Pushing the boundaries

Ripening and maturity – fruitful endeavours

Investing time in joining with others

Allowing yourself to be vulnerable and playful

Building on strong ties in the community, family and with significant others around you

Having a 'hosting' mindset – gathering others to eat and drink together

Paying attention to that moment of change when effort becomes transformation

Working the laughter muscles by seeing the funny side of things

Tending to what is flourishing as it reaches its crescendo of growth

Working from the heart by having conversations that truly make a difference

Summer for the outdoor gardener

Foliage is at its finest. Colour is everywhere. Summer fruits such as strawberries and raspberries are ripe and ready. Poppies, peonies and roses step up and take their place at the front of the stage. The garden at twilight is beautiful, peaceful and tranquil, with the scent of some plants now evident in the early evening stillness. There are birds everywhere and the night singers like the robin, blackbird, song thrush and the sadly rapidly declining nightingale can be heard.

Some key tasks for Summer:

- Checking methods for watering
- Tidying up perennials after flowering
- Cutting back perennials and taking cuttings
- Pruning flowering shrubs, deadheading roses after blooming
- Controlling with vigilance large hedges like Leylandi
- Watching for tomato problems
- Planning autumn vegetables
- Tackling weeds and mowing

Summer in the garden of life

The flame and fire of Summer shows up energetically in us too and offers us something different to ponder than in previous seasons. On the one hand, Summer is a time of community and relationships, be that with family, significant others, friends or colleagues. Building stronger partnerships and initiating acts of celebration for what is flourishing around us are important. The fire of Summer is concentrated on a sense of full-hearted joy and active play and the light and love of being alive.

The energy is moving ever outward into full maturity and dénouement. We can be ambitious, bold and daring. Passion and fireworks are for what we love to do: whether it is an exciting project, enticing goals and commitments or working on shared endeavours. The balance point is having enough flame to burn brightly and be expansive and not burn out when the fire is not tended properly. A good fire needs both fuel and air to burn brightly once ignited.

Summer is a time to rekindle fires too. It is about making extra time for friendships that are meaningful, being with family, or in community participating in activities that are important to where you live or work, which need extra boosting and strengthening,

Summer is ripe, loving, sensual and maturing energy. It is a season for spontaneity and openhearted joy as well as the fun and laughter connected with childlike play time. In our work-focused culture we tend to downplay pure enjoyment, play for playing's sake, not to compete or compare. So lay a picnic cloth in your own back garden and have a tea party!

Another aspect of Summer in the garden of life is that this is a season of passion, intimacy, sensuality and sexuality. This might manifest as encouragement to be adventurous, creative and spontaneous in your intimate relationships but that is not the whole of it. Sensuality is a connection to the senses for you as an individual, as well as part of a couple.

In the outdoor garden, planting took place in Spring and now this is a period of regular activities of tending and deadheading, feeding, watering, and mowing, if there is grass. Some of the frenetic activity, until harvest, has slowed down and a window of opportunity can be found to just sit in the splendour of your garden for a little while and enjoy your hard work. In the garden of life, this might be a great time to book a massage or a treat for your body that you might have overlooked earlier in a busy year, and can be a good way to evoke the seasonal spirit of Summer. Go swimming and really feel the smooth cool water on your body. Take the time to savour a favourite meal or indulge in the finest example of your favourite food; combine it with your favourite music perhaps?

Intimacy is an important quality for our times. Besides a sexual connotation, there is a much wider importance for all of us in what it means to be intimate in everyday life. It is all too easy to disconnect from the people around us as we make our daily way in the wider world. We often do not make eye contact with those who pass by us, like the barista who serves us in the coffee shop, the stranger who holds the door for us or us for them. Too much of the time in the digitised world around us, we keep our eyes fixed to the smartphone in our hand as we sit on the bus or train.

When we allow another human being into our space by engaging with them, for even a second or two, there is maybe a millisecond of 'we' and this connects us, however briefly, in the midst of our everyday routines. The times when I have noticed increased commuter kindness have been in the face of tragic events. I remember travelling on the bus and Underground trains just after the terrorist attacks in London in July 2005. For weeks afterward, everyone was extra polite, solicitous and patient towards each other. Everyone smiled and exuded a sense of compassion and support for those around them. We all had a common understanding that it could have been any one of us, or a loved one, and here we were, alive. Life is precious and impermanent. It created an intimate sense of community, just by travelling together. The same was true after the Paris Bataclan attack in 2015. It brought an Anglo-French intimacy that was incredible and almost visceral. But after a period of time the cycle of letting go and separating comes around again. Wouldn't it be good to have that sense of rallying warmth and kindness arise from something positive rather than from tragedy?

It can be all too easy for political rhetoric of any persuasion to reduce people or groups to 'them' and 'us': 'those' people, 'that' group. This separates us, often with the purpose of setting one group against another or in engendering fear of the other or even xenophobia.

When we do this we disconnect. Differences can appear threatening and we move further away from understanding each other. We don't catch the eye of the other person because we are too busy, too much in a hurry, too scared of what it will mean if we are really present to the other in front of us. We will get stuck, involved, bored, invaded or see our fear mirrored back to ourselves. Intimacy, in the largest sense, is an act of courage. To meet the gaze of another person can feel bold, strange. It makes us feel vulnerable too. We confuse looking with staring and shy away. Even with friends or colleagues, many people still avoid eye contact with those they know well. Yet we know from research in the book *A General Theory of Love*[9] that from the moment we are born, eye contact is a highly rated cue that tells us that we are connected to the other. Since the groundbreaking work by Giaconda Pizzolatti,[10] who discovered mirror neurons, we have learned that parts of our brain light up when we see other people perform what is called an 'intentional action'. We see something and we can understand what is happening for them and it affects us, like seeing someone in a movie cry and we feel moved to tears too. Mirror neurons are the brain's way of knowing what that state is in others and that makes it easier to collaborate. When we are connected in thoughts and emotions, we release oxytocin. It is the same chemical a small child gets when in physical contact with its mother or caregiver from the moment of birth. Oxytocin is released too when people dance together, play music together or engage in a collaborative or generative conversation. It is the neurochemistry for safe connectivity.

This is called limbic resonance. We rate it highly as a sign of trustworthiness when someone meets our gaze. When I see you and accept you as simply a human being trying your best to get on in the world, even if I do not agree with you, I share a moment of humanity with you, and this is intimacy.[11] When infants are born they can already detect minute changes in emotional responsiveness in the parent or caregiver. This capacity for limbic resonance that we develop is a mélange of mutual changes and adaptation inside us in relation to the other in front of us. In other words, we look to be understood and to understand the other person's state, and to see ourselves reflected through the gaze of another.

> "This we know, the earth does not belong to man; man belongs to the earth. This we know. All things are connected like the book, which unites one family. All things are connecting. Whatever befalls the sons of the earth we did not weave the web of life; man is merely a strand in it, whatever he does to the web, he does to himself."
>
> **Chief Seattle**

We are all connected, however thin the thread of this connection. We are all in our own imperfect ways striving to live a life of our choice and get on with each other in the best way we can throughout the adventure of being on this planet where all must live. We are like those sunflowers in the field turning our faces up to the sun with a definite 'yes, come what may'. Compassion deepens this connection and the intimacy of empathy that can arise through random acts of kindness.

Summer energy is full on. It is a season of abundance and passionate effort. It is a time of purposeful connection in relationship, whether with families, communities, or teams, seeking out those you might have lost touch with or who live a distance away.

The energy that rises up is different from the thrust of Spring bursting into being, still young and not yet fully formed, like a lamb finding its legs soon after birth. Summer energy is the celebration of life in its full display of colour and its deep connection with others. It is the embodiment of heart energy. You can move faster, accomplish more, and its aim is to grow, grow, and grow. It is full rounded and juicy but it can be sharp, angry and frustrated in the effort to get where it is going. Knowing how to manage this energy is important.

When you want to see the results of that effort flourish requires a combination of maximum outward engagement with well placed organisation. It is easy to get caught up in the push for the new, and frustrating if it doesn't happen as quickly as we would like. Pushing your limits is part and parcel of this season. Turn the heat down on worry and up on confidence, enhance self-esteem and glow. Don't hold back from life. Bring some physical or relaxing activity into the mix to balance the outward push.

"The reality for discovery consists not in seeking new landscapes but in having new eyes..."

Marcel Proust

Michael and Sarah

Michael and Sarah had been together for 15 years. Each worked as a solo entrepreneur, running two kinds of complementary consultancies, and they had both been equally successful in developing their businesses from the ground up. They managed their hours to allow for time off together, including one big trip a year somewhere far afield. They had an active social life as well as being of service to their local community.

They noticed that something was missing from their relationship that had been actively present in the earlier years, but they couldn't identify what it was. However, they knew they wanted it back and they wanted to be proactive about doing something about it.

Michael was very involved with his local church and he had been asked to take a bigger lead in the executive/administrative function. Sarah taught Sunday school on alternate weekends. They both enjoyed their commitment to the community but could see that it took up more and more of their time. Sarah played bridge once a week and was loathe to let her bridge partner down if she didn't turn up. Michael played golf once a week. It was fun and it was also a good source of contacts for his business. Before they knew it, Michael and Sarah had sped through a busy week, and every night one or the other, or both, fell asleep before 10pm.

Using the exercise **Walking the Sacred Circle** (see Chapter 11) Michael and Sarah explored the seasons of their relationship. Summer spoke most to them about their current needs. In order to pinpoint the places where they could make changes they also created a **Relational Heat Map** (also in Chapter 11) and identified things to do.

They shared stories special to them that held the flavour of past excitement and fireworks in their relationship. What became clearer as their stories unfolded was that their 'Summer season energy' had become depleted.

Once Michael and Sarah established that their preference for planning could serve them well, even if the plan was sometimes to have no plan, they felt excited about starting.

So when things are at their height, taking a step back and getting a sense of the bigger picture of what is at play can help us see what may be right in front of us but obscured by other activities. Like garden plants that become overgrown almost at the drop of a hat, they are thriving so much that another plant we were so keen on when we planted it in May, growing at a slower speed than its neighbour, is now somewhere underneath struggling to get some light. Whatever is big and juicy, what is largest or loudest, often demands more time and attention. The smart gardener, aware of this, makes sure that what is wanted and needed in the garden gets attention, whatever it needs, and even some tough love.

Stopping and taking stock of where you are in the midst of all the activity can be helpful and here are some activities that can help you do that. Choose whatever calls to you. Notice those that you feel resistant towards too, which can be a sign it would be good to try them.

Four Summer exercises

Intimacy large and small

Over the next few weeks, as Summer unfolds, look for two ways per week that you can offer a random act of kindness to someone. It is likely to be something that arises in the moment and may have no follow up at all. For example, offering to pick up a prescription or dry cleaning for someone who finds it hard to get out of the house or simply treating a friend or colleague to a coffee. It doesn't mean you are committed to a weekly chore.

There was a trend that began a few years ago for 'paying forward' with a random act of kindness. One example was someone driving through a toll booth paying for themselves and the person behind them. There was no opportunity to be thanked because the first driver was already gone by the time the second driver pulled up to the booth. 'Paying it forward' doesn't have to mean literally paying for someone else but it does mean passing forward goodwill and kind acts and looking for opportunities to do so in the moment. See how creative you can be, with a sense of fun and lightness. Find different opportunities to go out of your way for someone for no other reason than doing it. The mere act of looking for ways to be kind to someone may amaze you with what turns up...

Speaking from the heart

Being heartfelt is part of Summer's flavour. Here are some ideas:

1. Write it and say it: Think of someone who means a lot to you. Journal about how this person is important to you and how they make you feel. What qualities does he or she have as a person that you especially appreciate? Pick a time that seems right and tell them.

2. Mend it: There may be a relationship in your life where a rift has occurred and it has become metaphorically overgrown with weeds, obscuring the goodness that was once so evident. Perhaps one or both of you have been too busy or have procrastinated. Consider taking time to talk to them about how your relationship might be rekindled.

3. See it afresh: Call to mind someone you really need to talk to about something that is very important to you, or to both of you, but so far you have not found your voice or the best way into the conversation. Think about the situation from their perspective and how they see the world, as well as from your own perspective. What could you, on reflection, learn about them and their needs that might help you find the best way to engage in conversation with them? What might help increase understanding and co-appreciation? It can be an opportunity to check out any assumptions you may have made that has reinforced your own position, and to explore what else could be true.

Make a play date

Invite the energy of being at our ease, and invite the joy of the inner child, or that part of us that can cut loose without being overly concerned, even for a while, about the 'why' of what we do in favour of the pleasure of play.

During this season make a date with yourself once a week. Ringfence two or three hours a week and do something that is as far from work as you can think of. Pick something that is not already a regular activity, i.e. if you play tennis once a week then use your play date to do something else.

Maybe you'll pick something that you used to like doing as a kid, something you never did as a kid and always wanted to try, or something else that feels unserious, fun, an adventure even!

Some ideas:

Walk around an art shop, or toy store, or fine food deli you have always wanted to go to and spend an hour exploring as if you were an artist, or an eight year old or a chef, or something else far from your everyday self.

Spend an hour sketching, work with clay or pastel sticks to just draw. Don't worry about the output, just have a go!

Lie on your back in the garden and watch the clouds.

Go fishing or canoeing.

Find a garden or park to visit and have tea there afterwards.

Walk around a town you have never visited before.

Visit a museum you have never been to.

Get out an old board game or jigsaw puzzle and invite someone to play with you.

Go to a funfair and ride on something a little bit scary but exhilarating.

Heat up your love life

Is it time for a little more boldness? Think about how this might manifest and commit to experimenting with your partner. No partner at the moment but feeling sexy? How about a trip to buy some new underwear? This might sound like a girls' only trip but it is not unheard of these days for guys to have a wider choice in interesting undergarments. Be outrageous! Pick something that makes you feel like your best self or makes you smile. Maybe it's a colour or a style that makes you feel good in your body. No one has to know except you.

Greenhousing moment

Memory and our ability to do our best thinking are also linked to the element of fire. When you are in flow state this is especially true. Flow state is when we are so engrossed in what we are doing we seem to lose track of time. We become one with the task in such a way that we are at our best but almost unaware of what we are doing in separate minute by minute movements; rather it is a fluid state of being and doing at once. How have you experienced flow, and when?

Practices for Summer

1. Do the things that bring you joy. This is the time to linger longer over a night sky full of stars, the sun setting on a warm night, the intricacies of a stunning flower, holding hands with someone you love and relishing the moment just for what it is. Spend time in the sunshine, recharging your batteries to help you carry light and memories of warmth throughout the year.

2. Spend time with people who make you laugh. Cultivate the habit of appreciating and spotting the humour in the human condition.

3. Get outside and play a sport or find a friend to teach you one or go with you to learn.

4. Join a group that follows an interest of yours. Consider fun as important to your well-being as work or anything else you do.

5. Take care of important connections with others in your life. Think about where you need to invest time, effort and imagination into them. Reach out warmly to family and friends, putting aside any disagreements and old hurts.

6. Use touch more consciously. Research shows hugging reduces and relieves stress by releasing oxytocin.[12] Hug those you love more often. Old people in care homes often say the thing they miss the most is the simple act of touch, on an arm, a shoulder, a hug or holding a hand.

7. Look around at what you planted in Spring. Tend them well, nourish them as they ripen and flourish into their fullest potential. Make the most of your gifts and skills, as you step fully into a season of sharing the gifts of who you are. Nature is expanded to its fullest in the Summer. What was once seen as potential in the Winter is now manifesting in the Summer – the butterfly, once larvae, spreads its wings and shares its beauty in this season. Allow yourself to sparkle and to encourage the spark in others.

8. Work from the heart. Recall your passions; use Summer to bring your work or interests to a new level of expression and exposure. Discern what is valuable for you to continue doing and give it your wholehearted enthusiasm. If you don't know what your special passion is, stay amused and engaged in life and don't stop looking. Think about what 'working from the heart' means to you.

9. Connecting with someone you work or live with could involve a heartfelt conversation about the following:

    *   What do you share a passion for?

    *   What can we trust each other to uphold?

    *   Is there something we need to understand better between us before we can proceed?

    *   How can we grow or deepen our trust?

    *   What is the larger task we are involved in?

10. Take up laughter yoga. There are many sources in the UK and across the world. Learn more at http://laughterpilot.co.uk

> *If woman is inconstant, good, I am faithful to ebb and flow, I fall*
>
> *In season and now is a time of ripening.*
>
> Excerpt from 'Stepping Westwards' by Denise Levertov (*Poems 1960-1967*)

Meditation for a Summer evening

This is a lovely meditation to do outside on a warm Summer evening. Keep a blanket nearby so that you can stay warm as you sit. You might like to record this on your phone and allow time to pause between the sections. This meditation can take as little as 15 minutes or as much as a half hour. If you are not keen to listen to your own voice on a recording and would find it distracting, then ask a friend to record it for you. It is a lovely way to gather the voices you know and love to accompany your growing body of reflective exercises and meditations.

Let's begin. Make yourself comfortable... Let your body weight sink into the seat... Relax your body and close your eyes. As you bring your awareness inside, it can help to also bring kindliness to your awareness. Imagine a great open sky above your head and the curve and shape of a smile held within this vast space.

Imagine that curve and shape of a smile inside you, by the corners of your eyes, and let the corners of your mouth curve to a slight smile. As you breathe take that smile shape and imagine it in your heart. (*pause...*)

Allow yourself to connect with the sounds of Summer around you. What can you hear just nearby? If you take your hearing further away, what then... and further still...? Rest a few moments and just be receptive to the sounds all around you. (*pause...*)

Now bring your attention to your breath and notice where you feel it most strongly in your body. It could be in your abdomen, your chest or perhaps in the cool air coming in and out of your nostrils.... Enjoy its power and simplicity as the breath of life comes into you with an inhalation and out of you with an exhalation. Follow the breath in and out for a few moments... (*pause...*)

If you have any tension points in your body, and it is possible to let go a little more, do so. (*pause...*)

Now direct your inner attention to imagining a large garden of gorgeous flowers. It is a perfect Summer day, with a clear sky dotted with white clouds and a warm gentle sun filling the scene with light. The flowers are fragrant and abundant, their petals slightly moving in the pleasant and light breeze in the garden.

There is a path ahead not far away, meandering through a field of wildflowers. You follow this path, slowly and leisurely, feeling your feet making contact with the ground. You feel relaxed as you sense the beauty around you and in the life within you.

As you come to the end of this path, your heart is at peace. A little way ahead you see a small copse of magnificent trees and a small, still lake. Under an oak tree, on the edge of the lake, there is a clearing and a bench. A small campfire is lit and seems well tended. It glows a yellowy-crimson. Make yourself comfortable there. Your fire is of oak and fir tree branches and right beside it is a pouch containing the fragrant herbs of lavender, chamomile, and thyme. You empty these pouches into the fire, holding the thought of some negativity you may have in your life, and in the rising fragrance feel that it has been cleansed. (*pause...*)

As this is Summer the sun is taking its time to set. The sky is blue and pink; an Impressionist canvas of Mother Nature expressing all her creativity. Sit here for awhile if it feels right to do so. Her grand design is reflected on the stillness of the lake beside you. When you look at the lake, you see that it is a reflection of your life, and on its surface you are able to see, or experience, all the parts of who you are and what you are. Your soul's beauty, vastness and great love blend with the sunset colours and the pond's liquid shimmer. (*pause...*)

When you are ready, choose a stone or a pebble from on the ground around you. Holding it in your hand, make a promise to yourself about how you will honour the beauty inside you and what action you can take, or a thought you can hold that will live in the days and weeks ahead and even the year ahead until next Summer. One promise to yourself. When you have that in mind, launch the stone into the lake as a gesture of commitment to that promise.

When you are ready, follow your path back through the trees and the wildflowers. (*pause...*) As you come through the rose garden stop and choose a rose that you feel especially encapsulates what Summer is for you. Breathe in its perfume deeply. Imagine a name for it. (*pause...*) When you are ready, bring your attention back to your breathing. Follow your breath in and out for five more breaths at your normal pace.

When you are ready, open your eyes and return to the ebb and flow of everyday life around you.

Postcard from the Summer Hedgerow

Preparing for your weekly seasonal walks

1. First start by finding a place to sit or be at rest.

Take a few moments to get a sense of where you are. Become aware of where you are sitting or standing. Your feet should be flat on the ground, with your body balanced evenly between both feet. Shoulders are relaxed back and down and your spine erect but not rigid. Have your knees ever so slightly bent. If you are sitting have both feet flat on the ground, arms relaxed, perhaps in your lap. You may wish to drop your gaze down to the ground to remove any distractions or close your eyes if it feels comfortable for you to do so where you are.

Bring your attention to your breath and notice where you feel your in and out breathing most distinctly. It could be your abdomen, your chest, or the sensation of cool air flowing in and out of your nostrils. Follow the pace of your breath in and out without changing anything, just following it as it flows naturally for a few moments, perhaps a minute or two. Allow your body to release any tension.

When you are centred in yourself, reconnect with your body as it sits or stands where it is. Feel the holding solidness of the ground beneath your feet or the firmness of the chair or bench where you sit.

2. Consider your intention for your walk today.

You might choose a word or a quality or use one of the questions below as a walking prompt. If you do then let the question rest lightly as you walk, allowing whatever arrives in your head and heart to be. You can use the same questions over many weeks or choose a different one. You may notice different experiences presenting.

3. Use all of your senses.

When you are ready, begin your walk by holding openness to the qualities of the season in mind. Allow yourself to tune into what you can see, hear and sense on your walk – almost perhaps as if you were seeing it for the first time. Take time to notice. Move at plant speed.

Over the next weeks and months of the season pay close attention to newness as you walk, increasing your range of noticing what is new and fresh in you or in Nature, the parks and gardens around you as the season shifts day by day and week by week.

4. Give yourself a few uninterrupted moments to really look at something from every angle.

See it as if you had never seen one of its kind before in your life. Sniff it, touch it gently. Turn it over if you can. Close your eyes for a moment with it resting in your hand or on your finger. Think about its journey up to now and how it may have come into existence. Take in the nuance of its shade or colour, texture, line, and position.

5. Capture the essence at the finish for your Season's diary.

Use your *Postcard from the Hedgerow* to capture some words or a quick sketch, whatever suits you, that most helpfully summarises your walk. These cards, as the weeks go by, will be part of your weekly bite-size journaling. They capture a moment in time and are added to your collection as you travel through the year. Of course you may also want to write more but if you are new to journal writing this is a wonderful place to start because the space does not demand so much and they are very easy to carry with you anywhere.

Summer walks

This is the time of year to take advantage of the extra light and take a walk either before breakfast or after dinner. Find places that will take you to the smells of Summer that you like the most and luxuriate in being able to be outside without the additional layers of coats, hats and boots. Don't forget to take your journal and camera with you.

At the end of each of your walks take a little time to capture your immediate thoughts and feelings and the flavour of the walk on your *Postcard from the Hedgerow*. Create one after each walk. How they are different from your Spring walks?

Here are some Summer questions to reflect on as you take your weekly walks this season. Pick one per walk or several. Feel free to use the same question multiple times:

- What are you doing when you find yourself easily laughing and playing?
- When do you experience true and deep joy in what you do in your life?
- When do you allow yourself to be vulnerable, to reveal your tender side?
- In what ways are you ripening and maturing in thought or word or deed?
- How do you work in cooperation with others?
- Who are your dearest friends?
- What are the great passions of your life?
- Is your work taking you into new territory? Are you developing expertise and knowledge in something you are really interested in?

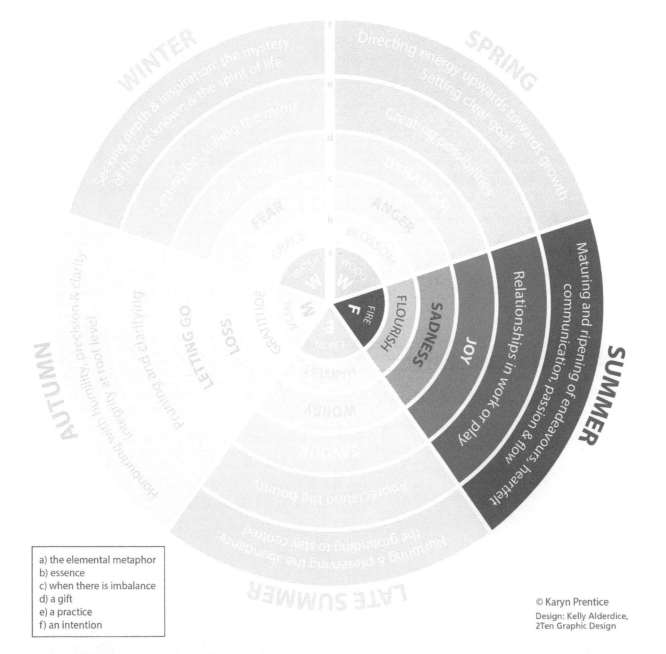

a) the elemental metaphor
b) essence
c) when there is imbalance
d) a gift
e) a practice
f) an intention

WINTER

Seeking depth & inspiration, the mystery of the not known & the spirit of life

Letting go, stilling the mind

SPRING

Directing energy upwards towards growth

Setting clear goals

Creating possibilities

DYNAMISM

FEAR

ANGER

GRACE

BLOSSOM

WATER   WOOD
W   W

W
W

METAL

FIRE
F

EARTH

GRATITUDE

FLOURISH

SADNESS

JOY

SUMMER

Maturing and ripening of endeavours, heartfelt communication, passion & flow

Relationships in work or play

AUTUMN

Honouring with humility, precision & clarity

Integrity at root level

Pruning and clarifying

LETTING GO

LOSS

WORRY

SAVOUR

HARVEST

Appreciating the bounty

Nurturing & preserving the abundance

the grounding to stay centred

LATE SUMMER

© Karyn Prentice

Design: Kelly Alderdice,
2Ten Graphic Design

CHAPTER 5
late summer

Hold at the centre: contain and savour the harvest

Late Summer is characterised by cooler mornings but still quite warm days. Though the days are getting shorter, the quality of light is still stunning and the sunrises can be spectacular at this time of year.

What I love about late August and early September is picking the long-awaited fresh vegetables that seem to ripen overnight into ready-to-eat food. The tomatoes are coming into a redness that is mouth watering just to behold, never mind taste, and courgettes with their delicate yellow flowers that I always promise myself to try and stuff with some wonderful filling and still have not done so.

Late Summer in the garden is about gathering and savouring the harvest. It is about developing greater self awareness and connection to your deepest self.

Where we live in Normandy, people are very generous with their seasonal garden crops. Returning home from a day out, it is not unusual for me to find a bag of just-picked runner beans or beautiful beefheart tomatoes hanging on the gate post or a green submarine of a marrow lying by the wall. We all share the bounty so that it can be eaten and appreciated while it is in its just-ready ripeness.

Into the evening and night of Late Summer can be heard the sound of farmers cutting the hay. However late, we can hear the huge farm machinery moving slowly up and down the fields to harvest everything while the machine is in their temporary loan.

Qualities associated with Late Summer

Maturing

Preserving and conserving

Savouring

Noticing what is ripe

Staying grounded

Consideration/thoughtfulness

Being in service to others

Empathy

Loving what is

Appreciating others

Taking stock

Earth energy

Savouring and generous

Unifying and being together

Maturing and ripening

Maintaining ground

Empathic

Resources preserved

Signs of imbalance or that you have not spent enough time in this season

Rushing to judge

Being stingy

Feeling bitter

Giving up

Focusing only on what's missing

Poor yield despite efforts

Not paying attention to the results

The outdoor garden in Late Summer

The sole objective of any flowering plant is to produce seed. The quicker the faded flowers are removed from annuals, tender perennials and roses the more they will produce.

This is the time to harvest the crops as they ripen almost daily. It is time to get the greenhouse ready for what will be overwintered and where you grow bedding and raise new crops. In the fields the hay and barley are being gathered. All the tender and attentive care of feeding fruit and vegetable plants throughout Spring and Summer is now paying off. There is nothing like eating something just picked from the garden!

Many gardeners take this abundance and share it, preserve it, freeze it and of course eat it, all the better shared with friends and family. There is something very satisfying about sharing a good crop with others. Late Summer in the garden is about tasting and savouring the abundance of our efforts and not passing through this stage too quickly. Everything that is harvested has been through effort expended, indoors and out.

Some key tasks for Late Summer:

- Sow tender perennials for a late display

- Seed a new lawn

- Make sure what can be safe all winter is cared for in storage

- Deadhead roses to stimulate more flowers

- Prune trained fruit late in season

- Overhaul the borders late in the season

- Store marrows and squashes for winter

- Protect, pick and store tree fruits

Late Summer and the element of earth

The rising heat of mid-August points to the end of the growing season. The air has a different feel, the nights are getting a wee bit longer and there is a perceptible chill in the night air that was not there in June and July. Growth is slowing, crops are ready and soon the harvest will be gathered.

We can look at what has been accomplished, hopefully with a feeling of satisfaction (from the Latin word 'sates', meaning 'being enough', and 'facture', meaning 'to make'). Our efforts have been prescient if we have taken due care and paid attention through the previous months.

What has come to fruition at this point for you? What is your harvest?

This is the time of year to start raising awareness about the change of rhythm, to slow down and pause between your many endeavours, and to reconnect with the natural cycle of life.

Mother Earth in Chinese medicine stands for generosity, thoughtfulness, and caring. It is a solid home ground, holding seeds of potential. This includes nourishment through the roots up to the branch tips. It helps us be strong and aids emotional sustenance.

How do you feed your mind and how do you feed your spirit? How do you stay centred and balanced with integrity?

This time of year is about being a supportive and trustworthy partner in the business of being human with our closest friends and family, with colleagues, with the environment and with Nature itself.

Reflection: What needs harvesting from last year? Where do you need to give thanks to someone or for something?

The gift of harvest

Late Summer is a time to gather and examine what we have grown in the year. To do this, we need to take our time to reflect and note what went well, appreciating the fruits of our labours, and linger over these in order to really remember and register them inside us. Rick Hanson, in his book *Hardwiring Happiness*, writes about building the habit of making the most of the positive experiences we have and encouraging ourselves to really connect with them so we can 'download the good' with a simple and effective process.[13] Many of us are very skilled in reviewing and ruminating over something that went wrong, embellishing it or making it bigger than it actually was. Hanson says this is not unusual. Our ancestors' survival depended on looking out for something bad that might happen in order to take action. The brain evolved a negativity bias that makes it less adept at learning from positive experiences but efficient at learning from negative ones. The good news is the skills we use to imagine a negative outcome are exactly the same as those needed to dwell longer on a positive one. We all just need practice. And it is those positive events, however small, we want to harvest for when we need to remind ourselves, and others, of our own capabilities.

The gift of harvest is to take the time to gather these with care and name them for ourselves and to share our harvest experiences with others. The business of being human is a complex one and a good harvest helps sustain us through tougher and leaner times.

Savour

Key to all this is to build our savouring muscles. Savouring is taking the time to really be with a good experience you are having so that you can appreciate it slowly and with intentional attention. The speed at which modern life operates is condensed too much into microwave happenings. We have soundbites, tidbits and 'nano-experiences'. Televisions are on simultaneously with telephones, laptops and music. These all have a relevant place at the table of life. Savouring is the opposite. To savour is to slow down and take time. To pause and enter fully into an experience, as near as possible to 100 percent. In the act of savouring we connect to the ground and centre ourselves so we can fully appreciate something, whether it is food, music, a scene in front of us, or the feel of something wonderful. We are allowing ourselves to be totally present.

Late Summer intentions in the garden of life

Nurturing and preserving the abundance

Staying grounded and centred

Taking the time to appreciate our efforts, skills, capabilities
and those of others

Recognising abundance all around us

Pausing and taking stock

Enjoying small pleasurable activities that take little effort
but nourish the heart, mind and soul

Making the most of our endeavours

Robert's Late Summer

Robert felt hard done by. He could be described as a 'glass half full' guy. When he looked at his life, his friends and his family, he saw what was missing, not what was there. If someone said 'isn't it a lovely day?' he would respond with 'it will probably rain soon'. Robert didn't say these things to be mean spirited. He felt it was always better to not be too optimistic and then he wouldn't be disappointed if things didn't work out. When we began to work together he had volunteered for the biggest project his parish council had ever taken on and he was not settling down well. He saw his role was to bring a 'reality check', as he put it, into the planning phase of the project he was a part of. He wanted to do right by the community and that it fell to him to be the nay-sayer so that all the possible contingencies could be taken into consideration. So why didn't anyone seem to like him? And how come this strategy that had helped him in his regular job was not very helpful now? We explored his way of seeing the issue through the lens of the Five Seasons.

Try this exercise:

Savouring is part of Late Summer energy.

The following is a well-known mindfulness exercise called 'the raisin meditation'. I have borrowed this version I especially like from Dr Ronald D. Siegel, Assistant Professor of Clinical Psychology, Harvard Medical School, from his book *The Mindfulness Solution*.[14] Before you begin, get yourself a couple of raisins and a little dish. If you have an aversion to raisins you can substitute them for a tangerine segment or perhaps a dried apricot.

Select a single raisin and place it in the palm of your open hand. Carefully examine it with your eyes. Notice its texture, colour and patterns. See where it is shiny and where it is full. Notice, too, any thoughts or feelings that arise as you hold it.

Next, use your thumb and forefinger to explore the raisin's texture (you might wish to close your eyes for this to better concentrate on the touch sensations). Observe its hills and valleys, whether it is soft or hard, smooth or rough.

Once you have explored it thoroughly in your hand, remain aware of the sensations of your arm moving through space and lift the raisin to your ear. Hold it just outside of your ear canal and roll it between your thumb and forefinger, exerting a little bit of pressure. (Resist any urge that may arise to insert the raisin in your ear!). See if you can hear the faint sound a raisin makes as you manipulate it.

After listening to the raisin for a few moments, slowly and consciously bring it beneath your nostril. Breathe in and see if you can detect any raisin aroma. Also notice your feelings in reaction to whatever you smell – do you find it pleasant, unpleasant, or neutral?

Inhale deeply several times to really take in the smell of the raisin.

Now bring the raisin in front of your lips and allow your tongue to reach out and capture it. Just let the raisin lie between your tongue and the roof of your mouth for a while. Notice any reactions that your mouth has. Notice again any feeling responses that arise. Continue to cradle the raisin like this for a moment or so.

Next, begin to use your tongue to explore the raisin. See how these sensations are similar to, or different from, those you experienced when exploring it with your thumb and forefinger. Notice also how the raisin changes as it spends more time in your mouth.

Once you feel that you have thoroughly explored the raisin with your tongue (do take your time) gently position it between your upper and lower molars. Just hold it there for a bit and see what that feels like. Notice any urges to bite down, or perhaps even to protect the raisin.

Now, allow your molars to come together once – but only once. Observe what happens. Notice whatever taste sensations, urges and feelings rise. Just stay with the experience of the raisin crushed between your teeth as your mouth and mind react to it.

Next, use your tongue to capture the raisin again and explore your handiwork. See all of the ways in which it has changed and notice how it continues to change as you explore it further. Once the raisin has fallen apart, allow yourself to continue chewing, noticing all the different sensations and urges that arise. Observe your swallow reflex and how the sensations in your mouth continue to change.

Wish the raisin well as it continues its journey down your alimentary canal.

31-day Savour exercise

Using your journal or your camera, write once a day about something you savoured each day. Your prompts are opposite:

1. Morning
2. Trees
3. People
4. Place
5. Animal
6. Taste
7. Sounds
8. Story
9. Colour
10. Laughter
11. Family
12. Kiss
13. Book
14. Art
15. Music
16. Memory
17. Comfort
18. Excitement
19. Night
20. Friendship
21. Gift
22. Fulfilment
23. Film
24. Gratitude
25. Giving
26. Receiving
27. Finding
28. Warmth
29. Surprise
30. Contentment
31. Arrival

Robert

Robert felt that all his working life, he had strived to get as much done in as short a time as possible. The memory of his mother's voice saying 'there's always a problem lurking' meant he was always on alert for what might be missing or could present a problem. The season that was most keenly missing for Robert was Late Summer. He realised that he did very little savouring. He rushed his meals to get on with the next thing to do, and rarely listened to music, hearing it instead as 'background sound'.

Mostly, he shocked himself to find that he had no sense of what was 'enough' or sufficient; he was always looking for 'more' or 'different' from what he had.

Robert created a regular practice of appreciating, observing and noticing the good things around him and in others. He worked through a number of practices that helped him connect more to his senses. Gradually he found the committee were more open to hearing his generally good suggestions for improvement because he was beginning to balance them with more genuine recognition of what other people did or brought to the table. Starting those practices allowed him to build a reserve of goodwill and collaboration that he had been missing.

Late Summer practices

Harvest/ripening – This is the season to really take stock of all that you have received over the year or over longer periods. The timeline exercise in Part 2 will help you identify all the fruits above the line – successes, gains, wins, joys.

Your own garden at home may be bursting with fruit. You may have neighbours or friends with an orchard. Joining with the communal effort of bringing in the harvest is an ancient collective process. It is one of the reasons that communities survived, by helping each other with the harvest when all the fruit of the year was ready and ripe all at once.

Abundance – looking at your life with an attitude of abundance rather than that of scarcity. How at ease are you with seeing through the lens of abundance? Notice how that impacts on your well-being in all senses of the word. It is much easier to be generous, considerate and flexible from a position of abundance. And the letting go of Autumn flows more easily when we believe that we have all that we need.

Nourishment – take time to prepare and enjoy your food. Whether you eat alone or with others in this season, take time to lay a nice table, and enjoy each mouthful mindfully. Try to eat without the distraction of a TV, a computer or a book. Enjoy a meal with your friends or family and in a relaxed way without hurrying off as soon as the food is gone. Allow time for digestion by slowing down and really tasting the food.

Gathering – make a centrepiece for your table with accumulated bounty from the garden, be it flowers, fruits or grasses. Create your own ritual for really savouring what is still fruiting and being nourished by you and for you.

Alignment and centring – when life is very busy it is easy to lose the alignment of our energy. We get drawn into many activities, demands and tasks so that we give a little energy here, another bit over there and, overall, our energy and focus gets fragmented.

Develop a space to cocoon yourself even briefly for recharging your battery, just as we all do with our mobile devices. This might be a room itself or a place in a room that is special to you and that represents a different energy: a relaxed, quiet, sustained space to be in. It might be where you do some meditation regularly, or a special chair that is 'yours'. This may be where you grab some time to while away the day just by being in the moment, or to write in your journal.

This is a good season to include practices like yoga, T'ai chi, or long walks consciously connecting with the earth beneath our feet. Walking barefoot in your own garden increases awareness and helps us to connect with nature through our feet. What practices do you already have in place to keep yourself centred?

Nurturing can also be for others. Are you practised at being a nurturing presence to others? Provide an understanding and sympathetic ear for those you care about. Offer a helping hand to someone in need.

The diminishing light also impacts on the availability of vitamin D. Be aware of what your body needs, so walks and sunshine are good activities. Exercise that connects you to the earth – walking, climbing, even laying a picnic on the grass – brings us inevitably closer to Nature and the landscape.

Late Summer is a time to develop greater self awareness and connection to who you are and what your potential is. It is a season to look for the connection between what seeded in Spring and what has grown and ripened since.

Compliment someone on a talent that they have been using well. Identify one of your best talents and use it. Ask yourself: where do I see people I know growing and using their talents? How and in what ways can I recognise that I am growing as a person?

Harvest meditation

A full moon that appears within a week or two of the Autumn Equinox is sometimes called a 'Harvest Moon' and is often attributed to Native Americans like the Algonquins from north east United States. This was because it marked when corn was to be harvested. Most often, the September full moon is the Harvest Moon, which is the full moon that occurs closest to the Autumn Equinox. In two out of three years, the Harvest Moon arrives in September, but in other years it occurs in October.

At the peak of the harvest, farmers can work late into the night by the light of this moon because the Harvest Moon has an abundance of bright light and can be more colourful. The effects have to do with the seasonal tilt of the earth. The warm colour of the moon is caused by light from the moon passing through a greater amount of atmospheric particles than when the moon is overhead.

This meditation is designed to help you recognise and appreciate your gifts and find the magic of gratitude. Find yourself in a comfortable position somewhere you will not be disturbed. Relax by taking a few deep in-breaths and long slow out-breaths.

When you are ready, imagine that you are sitting at the head of a long oak table. Your chair is comfortable and throne-like. Around you, an imposing hall takes shape. The light is muted but there are candles lighting the spaces, alcoves and window ledges with a warm glow. There is a fire warming the space in a tall and wide fireplace. You smell the scent of wood-smoke. The word 'abundance' appears woven in a wall hanging facing you, its jewel-like colours attracting your eye.

You slowly become aware of voices and activity in the distance, approaching you. There is a banquet being prepared in your honour. People begin to come in and the table is being laid by attendants – additional candles are lit, plates are set out. Guests start to arrive. You notice the companions who sit near you and the people who serve you.

Minstrels enter and begin to play music. The music repeats the theme of abundance. What does it sound like? What is it saying? The minstrels are yours to command – what do you want them to sing?

Now food is being brought in. Luscious fruit – pies of all kinds as well as apples, blackberries, plums and pears, are piled on huge serving platters. There are rosy red tomatoes and root vegetables, like carrots, sweet potatoes, beetroot, and squashes of many colours and shapes. There may also be cereal crops like barley, wheat and maize. You reflect on the generosity of the earth and the magic of the soil that has yielded all of this. (*pause...*)

Now preserved produce is brought in – pickles and jams of all varieties. You find yourself reflecting on how it is possible to preserve so many of the earth's resources so that humankind can use them well and appreciate them.

You become aware of all that you have to be grateful for, large and small, in your life. The gratitude spreads through your being, warming you. (*pause...*) You remember more and more things to be grateful for, and you feel very rich and blessed... (*pause...*)

The minstrels fall quiet and all chatter stills. A robed figure is entering the hall. You realise that this is the most important part of the ceremony and that something is being given to you that is very personal.

The robed figure is carrying a small gold dish. As he or she approaches you see that there is something special on the dish. This represents your own personal 'harvest' – something that you can gather in, that can nourish you and empower you...Take some moments to see what this gift is and what it means to you.

You take your gift with thanks and music and feasting begins. You can stay with the scene a little while longer and when you are ready, bid the scene goodbye and take your leave, returning to everyday reality with the promise that you will practise the act of gratitude every day.

When you are ready, make a note of anything from the exercise that emerged for you.

Postcard from the Late Summer Hedgerow

Preparing for your weekly seasonal walks

1. Start by finding a place to sit or be at rest.

Take a few moments to get a sense of where you are. Become aware of where you are sitting or standing. Your feet should be flat on the ground, with your body balanced evenly between both feet. Shoulders are relaxed back and down and your spine erect but not rigid. Have your knees ever so slightly bent. If you are sitting have both feet flat on the ground, arms relaxed, perhaps in your lap. You may wish to drop your gaze down to the ground to remove any distractions or close your eyes if it feels comfortable for you to do so where you are.

Bring your attention to your breath and notice where you feel your in and out breath most distinctly. It could be your abdomen, your chest, or the sensation of cool air flowing in and out of your nostrils. Follow the pace of your breath in and out without changing anything, just following it as it flows naturally for a few moments, perhaps a minute or two. Allow your body to release any tension.

When you are centred in yourself, reconnect with your body as it sits or stands where it is. Feel the holding solidness of the ground beneath your feet or the firmness of the chair or bench where you sit.

When you are ready, begin your walk by holding an openness to the qualities of this season in mind. Allow yourself to use all of your senses. Tune into what you can see, hear and sense on your walk – almost perhaps as if you were seeing it for the first time.

2. Consider your intention for your walk today.

You might choose 'awareness', or a colour, or a feeling like 'peace' or 'curiosity'. Or you might choose to use one of the questions below as a walking prompt. If you do then let the question rest lightly as you walk, allowing whatever arrives in your head and heart to be. You can use the same questions over many weeks or choose a different one. You may notice different experiences presenting themselves each time.

Some questions to ponder on your Late Summer walks

Where is the abundance?

What is ripe and ready to harvest?

What can you appreciate?

What might you savour from the past month or year?

To whom do you show thoughtfulness?

How do you nourish yourself, and others?

Where is there safe refuge in your life?

What needs thoughtful tending right now?

How do you establish a solid footing or alignment with what is true for you?

What supports your self-esteem and strength?

What makes your heart sing?

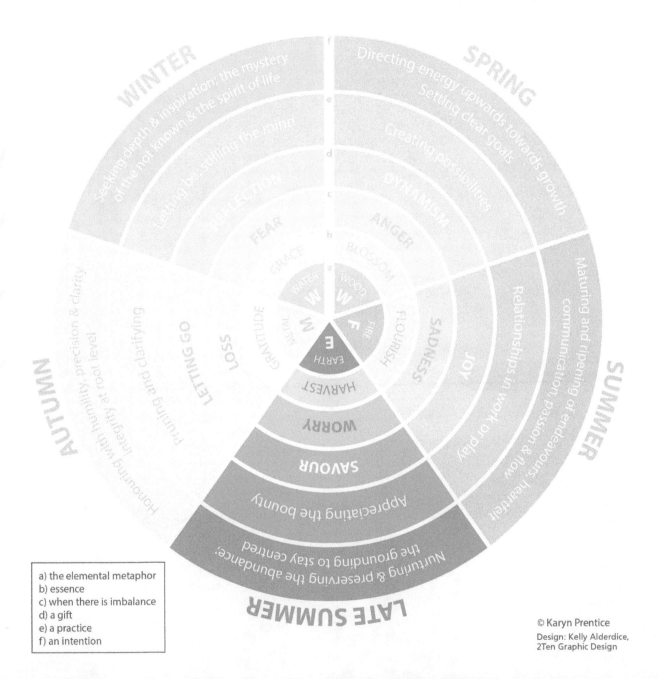

a) the elemental metaphor
b) essence
c) when there is imbalance
d) a gift
e) a practice
f) an intention

WINTER

Seeking depth & inspiration; the mystery of the not known & the spirit of life

Letting be; stilling the mind

REFLECTION

FEAR

GRACE

WATER

W

SPRING

Directing energy upwards towards growth

Setting clear goals

Creating possibilities

DYNAMISM

ANGER

BLOSSOM

WOOD

W

SUMMER

Maturing and ripening of endeavours; heartfelt communication; passion & flow

Relationships in work or play

JOY

SADNESS

FLOURISH

FIRE

F

AUTUMN

Integrity at root level

Honouring with humility; precision & clarity

Pruning and clarifying

LETTING GO

LOSS

GRATITUDE

METAL

M

E

EARTH

HARVEST

WORRY

SAVOUR

Appreciating the bounty

Nurturing & preserving the abundance; the grounding to stay centred

LATE SUMMER

© Karyn Prentice
Design: Kelly Alderdice,
2Ten Graphic Design

CHAPTER 6
autumn

There comes a moment in the garden when suddenly, almost as if overnight, the green leaves of our silver birch trees have switched from green to a mantle of gold and yellow. The Virginia creeper's Bordeaux red tones cut a breathtaking swathe over the back wall of the house. Accelerated by the wind, the trees are relinquishing their load. Now, a few weeks on, the display of rustic majesty has all but passed and our job is to collect the leaves that spread like draped silk around tree trunk bases and on top of flower beds everywhere in the garden. It is better for me than any visit to the gym, with all the stretching and bending, getting behind shrubs and under bushes, filling bag after bag of leaves.

It is already beginning to smell like Winter in the mornings. Wood being burned in chimneys, pine coming into its wintery best, cinnamon and orange fragrance in the air. I can feel a definite nip in the air, the cold tingles at the tip of my nose. In the flat lands where I live, there is often a very low mist over the fields that has risen from the ground in the early hours. The sun is much lower. The starlings and sparrows have all but finished stabbing away at the remaining figs that sit, like suspended dusky green marbles, on the tops of the fig trees, unwilling to give up and drop but no longer having either the strength or sunshine enough to arrive at that so sweet and delicious stage as those I collected a month ago. The burnished Cox apples and small conference pears are now gathered in, hurrah! At this time of the year my husband and I like to recognise and mark the passage of Late Summer into Autumn. We wrap up in the layers of fleeces and scarves we need in order to stay out for at least an hour and have an Autumn barbecue. Occasionally, I have resorted to gloves just to stay out there but this year it is beautiful, even in early November. We have had the last lunch on the deck (wearing our coats) before packing away the accoutrements of Summer outdoor living against the next month's harshness, and our final few cuppas sitting on the deck catching a late October stripe of sun. Two chairs and a bench remain for the hopeful of heart and hearty of disposition. You never know, do you?

This switch from Late Summer to fully fledged Autumn can catch us unawares in other ways too. We get busy again after Summer. The school term has restarted and all the chores and tasks that seemed so distant before Summer are right here. September to November can be very busy times. Before we know it, Winter celebrations beckon on the horizon.

Autumn in the garden outdoors is a time to honour and appreciate what the land has provided over the year. At the same time, it is when we decide what needs judicious pruning to encourage new growth and flourishing, and make space for new beginnings in the following Spring.

Some key tasks for Autumn:

- Autumn is a good time for planting trees, especially bare-rooted ones which is less stress for them
- Harvest apples and other crops
- Take hard wood cuttings while soil is still warm
- Plant up indoors containers for Winter and Spring
- Plant tulips and other bulbs
- Carry out winter pruning
- Protect plants against frost
- Put the lawn mower away until Spring

Autumn in the garden of life reminds us that it is important not to overlook the rituals of honouring in the moment what is right here now, as well as recognising the impermanence of all things. This sacredness of the rhythm of life is mirrored in Nature. Where can we go for our inspiration? Connect to our core values about what are, in essence, the most important lessons of the year? This is something we can do for the garden of our life. Perhaps we feel the overwhelm of too much to do, or the accumulation of what has become clutter. Now is a good time to clarify what is most important, what we must keep and what we must let go of, what we appreciate in our own ways so that, going forward, we are best placed to receive Winter's restorative energy as the end of the year approaches.

Autumn is about letting go and endings, which sometimes bring both a sense of awe and of grief. This is a challenge, especially when we want to hold on to everything. It is a time of choosing wisely with acknowledgement for what has gone before. We will also complete the largest cycle from birth to death. In Autumn we may be able to achieve much of wondrous value, as many do, in our various ways, in this later life season. It can be a healing time, an awakening, a reconciliation. It can be a time to say goodbye and to honour losses that have occurred during the year or indeed during our life.

Qualities associated with Autumn

Acknowledging our unique gifts, strengths and shortcomings

Letting go

Loss and impermanence

Getting to the essence of what is important

Respecting, honouring and treasuring

Feeling grief

Reconnecting with core values

Cutting away judiciously

Grit

Being with the sacredness of the rhythm of life

Awe and inspiration

Underscoring the preciousness of life

Taking time to appreciate our gifts

Understanding ourselves

Measuring what to keep and what to let go

Naming the essentials

Autumn and the element of metal

It can be useful to think of the elements as an interplay of energies critical to life on earth. When energies are in harmony and are strong and balanced, this helps life to flourish. When we take time to consciously and mindfully follow our breath in and out with a practice such as mindfulness, we too, as human beings, are adding to the flow of life; as oxygen arrives and carbon dioxide departs, so each breath puts us in touch with respect for all life.

According to Chinese practices, like acupuncture, metal is the element that most corresponds with Autumn. Metal stands for minerals and the air itself, which in turn facilitate the creation of water, Winter's element. Metal symbolises the value of all aspects of creation and our intrinsic value as human beings and who we are at the centre of our deepest selves. Human bodies contain minerals, including potassium, sodium, calcium and magnesium that, even in minute quantities, are essential for life.

Metal is very versatile. Most cultures treasure their country's precious metals. They can be melted and fashioned into other things. Emotional 'metal' also makes us strong, resilient and organised. Metal can be turned to liquid, made into a weapon or a building tool. It can break and it can protect. Your gifts, skills, and talents are the precious metals of your day-to-day garden of life. So we can work with our highest qualities and abilities with dignity and integrity to bring forth the unique expression of who we are.

In Autumn especially, as leaves fall, we are aware of letting go of what must die back or be pruned away, and we need to take time to clarify and name what is really most essential for life. Included in this process is reviewing what your values are and what will sustain you as you move into the coming Winter season. Our core values are at the heart of who we are and like minerals, come in all shapes, sizes and quantities. They are intrinsic to the meaning and purpose of how we live our lives. In Part 2 of this book, **Through the Gardening Lens**, you will have the opportunity to consider the soil in the garden of your life and to work on an exercise exploring your core values.

Signs of imbalance or that we have not spent enough time in this season

Experiencing difficulty in letting go

Being over-cluttered in one or more area of our lives

Stuck-ness or feeling like our energy is going nowhere or is blocked

Losing sight of what we value – not being able to see the wood for the trees

Holding fast and becoming rigid and over rule-bound (where we have lost sight of what the purpose of the rule was to begin with)

Going along with decisions made by others because we have lost a level of discernment

Losing connection with our self-esteem, even if temporarily

Reflection points:

In winemaking there is a gray fungus, known as *botrytis cinerea* or 'noble rot', which affects many plant species. However, for certain grape varieties, like Semillion and Riesling, exquisite wines can be produced using the impact on the grape of this fungus, that is often rare and costly. In life, there are exquisite moments we might miss because we are not alert and truly present to them before that moment has slipped away or is no longer viable. They may not always seem instantly attractive options but the gift is there. Luckily, in life we have more opportunities than the poor grape, or peach, to make the most of what is right here, right now.

Greenhousing moment

Looking back, when and where have you noticed a moment of change, a turning point you might just as easily have missed – and you didn't? What happened?

Cultivating Gratitude

Gratitude is a mindset. It is most associated with harvest time but the art of gratitude can be practised all year round. We need to step up and create more opportunities to appreciate and express our gratitude for what we have right here now beneath our noses and feet if we look. Bringing intentional attention to what is good right now builds memories which help us be more resourceful in lean times. Seasonally, we are preserving and conserving and digesting these good moments, to draw on them as September warmth gives way to Autumn's arrival. We can stock up our metaphorical cupboard with what we want to keep hold of and remember. If the act of being grateful calls to you in this season you can also visit the excellent website **www.gratefulness.org** for more inspiration on gratitude practices, inspiration and articles.

The gift of letting go

If we have done the groundwork of our Autumn intentions we have honoured what has come to pass and taken the good from it in. Now is the time to make choices about what needs to be cut away in order to support life and growth next year. Letting go is linked to creating space on the one hand, and also a bow of acknowledgment for all that was, and that which is not in our control to keep or hold on to. Autumn heralds a dying back, a dying away, and endings. We face loss. Everyone does. We don't get to choose to opt out. How we face it is our choice.

Autumn intentions in the garden of life are about:

Evaluating with precision

Knowing what to close down and what still needs discussion

Speaking our truth and learning the truth of others

Recognising the value of our, and others, contributions

Gratitude and appreciation of the journey so far

Honouring the best of what has gone before and letting go of what no longer serves

Pruning, removing the 'dead wood' so what can grow in Spring will have the space to do so

Clarifying our skills, accomplishments, gifts and talents

Being inspired about what we will see and plant for the next cycle

Gratitude

Geoffrey's Autumn

Geoffrey had been employed all his working life in the London head office of an international investment company, steadily rising up the organisational ladder. At 61 and in robust good health, he was a well-respected member of the senior management team, and as his retirement approached, he was given a lot of help and support in thinking about how he was going to hand over his responsibilities over the next 12-18 months. He had attended workshops on subjects such as his finances, his health and adjusting to a new schedule. He said on a bad day it felt like he was 'on a conveyor belt on the way down to the grinder'. On a good day, he knew that having free time would be a relief and that he was looking forward to not having to be tied up all day in meetings. 'But surely', he said when he came to see me, 'there must be more to life at this point? My wife says that I am in the autumn of my life and that it is just the way it is.' There was defeat in his voice. The question he wanted to focus on was: how might he frame his understanding and appreciation of this time of his life that could help him begin to think about 'what next?' in a fresh way?

Geoffrey reviewed the stories he was bringing with him about retirement, about what he thought he was capable of and what he dismissed for a range of reasons. He realised he was carrying not only his own ideas about what this next phase might be like but also carrying his own parents' and even grandparents' stories.

His story headline was 'It is all downhill after retirement'. When he took time to think about this, he recognised that people he knew reasonably well who had retired were living pretty good lives. Some travelled, some did not. Some were involved in voluntary projects and one or two had part-time work. Some spent time on different sports. There was no one in his immediate circle of friends who had 'given up' after they stopped work and did nothing at all. However, he realised that his grandfather had done exactly that – 'given up'. He had not survived more than six months after he retired. That had strongly influenced Geoffrey's father, who was nervous of retirement from almost middle age onwards. This story was not Geoffrey's but it had influenced him at a gut level. The story lived in the soil of his own roots and he paid more attention to that than to his immediate circle of peers. The more he unpicked his unquestioned beliefs about retirement, the more he felt like he was letting go of old baggage that he had not taken the time before to be conscious of, let alone question. He could enrich the soil of his understanding with different information that acted as nutrients to his own mindset by reflecting on a different set of questions, starting with:

What makes for a meaningful life and what does not?

What are your assumptions and beliefs about what is possible and what is not?

What stories might you be holding or telling yourself that need to be reviewed because they no longer serve you?

Greenhousing moment

Looking back, when and where have you noticed a moment when you needed to honour something important? What was it and why was it important?

Autumn in the garden of life

This season invites us to spend time immersed in conspicuous and purposeful deep appreciation of what has been good for the mind, body and soul over the year. In Nature, sap is beginning to move down into the roots. Taking time to acknowledge our strengths and the gifts we bring, as well as our shortcomings, are Autumn's call to salute the preciousness of life itself and also its impermanence.

In life's garden, Autumn is a good time to turn our attention to clearing up old but unresolved issues with others or within ourselves. Are the stories we tell ourselves about events in the past still serving us? Have we narrowed the version of the story and left out other information? What else could be true?

We can choose to become more conscious of where we are holding onto old emotional pain. However true those feelings are or were, the unnecessary suffering we continue to hold on to may well need to be put to rest, while honouring what has been hard and challenging. By 'unnecessary' suffering, I mean the kind that we create for ourselves. With appropriate attention, kindness and compassion we can see our experiences with a fresh set of eyes and give ourselves space to be bold, courageous and creative.

All too often we can become hostage to our stories about what we think is going on when there is probably a lot more information potentially available that we don't pay attention to. The more we repeat the story about an event to ourselves the more that single story becomes lodged in our mind as 'the truth'. Other facts become fainter until the story, plus all the feelings associated with it, becomes the only version we hold on to. How we explain events in our lives to ourselves can help us stay focussed and positive or make us unhappy, regardless of what actually takes place. Autumn is a good time to clear our thinking, as much as our cupboards and drawers, to check out whether our stories are serving us or if we need to let them go or revise them.

The outdoor garden in Autumn

Tree planting happens through November, especially bare-rooted trees, as this is a time of the least stress on a new tree. Plants can put all their energy into making new roots while the soil is still holding some of its Summer warmth. After losing their leaves, deciduous trees and shrubs actually have a surge of root growth. Evergreen are slightly different. They drop leaves continuously a few at a time so growth never stops, so it is also a good time to plant these.

Beside clearing space in the outdoor garden, it is time to dig the soil and add to it nutrients like compost, or appropriate organic matter. Bacteria breaks it down further and plant foods are released into the soil. This encourages earth worms as they are part of the cycle of life in the garden and therefore there are dual benefits from their presence. Mulching and digging now is something that will help the garden in the Winter nights to come.

Leaf mould is a wonderful, crumbly material that looks something like peat and has lots of goodness. A mini shot of this down a seed drill before sowing helps seeds nest in a tiny cosy duvet, germinating strong seedlings that will be raring to go.

In the garden of life we can be busy with these kinds of tasks too. Harvesting our best efforts, and the things we have brought to life during the growing seasons, whether ideas, projects, or relationships, captures the satisfying moments of the year. It is important to take the time to properly express gratitude and appreciation of what has been created, and not in a cursory way. The savour of Late Summer transforms now into something on a deeper level. It also acknowledges loss and grief and saying goodbye until the next cycle of growth in Spring brings with it new hope.

Thinking ahead to what we want to bring into our life over the next year means taking time now to evaluate carefully the space that is needed for it and what must be pruned or removed. Life may be full but the agile life gardener must bring a finely-tuned eye that can hold both what is visible now and imagine what is to come when Winter becomes Spring. At this time we see sheltering and protecting of nascent ideas that are still in the 'what if?' phase of development and require tender attention while they gather strength over Winter. Before the energy has gone to ground, the life gardener must attend to his or her well-being. This is the soil and roots of who we are and its resilience and robustness needs enriching as much as the good earth surrounding the plants and bulbs we have planted.

This means when we go deeper to nurture ourselves, we feed the future of who we will become in the next cycle of 12 months and beyond. There may be painful moments to revisit, tasks that help us enrich the ground of who we are, and that help us discern what is really important, necessary and vital going forward – and what is not.

Taking action

Signs of burnout and stress are commonplace in the modern, Western world. The idea of slowing down and resting is all too often relegated to wishful thinking. Resilience-building programmes are more commonplace in organisations these days but are taught in bite-sized chunks so as not to impact negatively on employee productivity. The quantity of work each employee must produce is still sky-high. Stillness and slowing down need to be recognised as more than wishful thinking because the impact on human beings is devastating. Something else needs to happen. And in some quarters it is. The number of books on the importance of slowing down, and taking the time to be mindful has grown substantially over the last ten years. There are literally hundreds of them if you go to an online book seller. A few are listed in Chapter 11.

In daily life we may not be so attuned to the season's energies. Not paying attention to the particular season can add to a sense of feeling out of sorts and out of rhythm. When we miss out one part of the five-stage cycle, when we race through it without intentional attention, there are potential risks. In the case of Autumn, doing too much and for longer hours, metaphorically speaking, is not seeing the wood for the trees. People are continually tired because they are out of balance in their energy expenditure versus replenishment. We simply lose our way.

Geoffrey thought he couldn't be the only person experiencing these feelings so he took a chance and reached out across the entire organisation to others who, like him, were in the 12-month countdown to retirement. He invited them to a coffee morning as a gathering place for support and sharing during this transition, and here the Go FAR (Further after Retirement) group was born. They gathered monthly over coffee or lunch and encouraged each other to explore ideas and plans for after they left the organisation. Geoffrey began chairing it, and then several others took turns. He remained friends with a few members long after the original group disbanded.

Geoffrey began looking forward to having more time to just potter and not be on the treadmill as he had been for a long time. At the same time, the vagueness of the future exacerbated his need for structure: 'I don't want to be bored'; 'I don't want to do something that feels like my job but for no money, however worthy the cause'; 'I don't want to be tied down'; 'I don't want to continue working with figures, just because that's what I am good at.' All of Geoffrey's 'don't wants' left little space to explore what might be possible.

It was as though as he picked up ideas here and there; alone and with his group, he was gathering up the fallen leaves of Autumn. The more his hands were full, the more the leaves slipped back down, only to be scooped up yet again. All the time he was metaphorically bending down to pick up leaves, he couldn't even begin to see where he was going – he felt he needed to stay busy. The leaves on the ground were not going to be wasted. In gardening terms, leaves become the mulch for what grows below the ground, or they go into the compost bin to nourish somewhere else in the garden the next season, or the one after.

Realising he would benefit from learning to let go of his old work-style pace in favour of something different, Geoffrey decided he might wrap up the tender shoots of ideas he was exploring and overwinter them, like a gardener would do some plants. He had time to mull over what new activities to pursue until Spring and give himself the luxury of time to celebrate the past 35 years of his career in the City.

Geoffrey began a scrapbook for all the clippings and the newsletter items he had produced at work, and photos of when his team had won national awards. It made him sad that he wouldn't be involved anymore and he was also proud of his contribution. He decided to write to a few members of his team individually before he left.

It made him realise how much time, effort, and skills he had built up and brought into his working life when he saw it all in the spread of his scrapbook pages. He had enabled two generations of young adults, as they moved up and onwards into some terrific careers in and outside his organisation. He felt renewed in that he had made a difference and that he had talents and gifts to offer elsewhere, albeit in a different form.

He looked at what he was glad to prune away from his daily life and how the extra space would allow him to rekindle some friendships that he hadn't made time for when he was so busy. He decided he would give himself some research time over the Winter to explore possibilities before making any final choices.

Geoffrey realised a good de-cluttering of his own thinking made a difference and that was just the start. The team was under great pressure with everyone doing more than their contracted hours to try and meet all the deadlines. The team rarely took time to recognise and appreciate the supreme effort everyone made collectively and individually. The home-unfriendly timetable was taken as the organisational norm. He decided to set up a 'Friday appreciation of the week' citation as a little way of recognising how important their contribution was to the project and to the organisation. Everyone was encouraged to nominate an action by someone that they appreciated during the previous week.

Leaving space that was unfilled by activity felt a bit scary at first for Geoffrey because he wanted to rush in and fill it all up. We looked at the concept of Wu Wei or 'The Fertile Void'.[15] In Chinese tradition this space was called 'fertile emptiness' because contrary to being empty, it was a space of potentiality, waiting for whatever arrived there; for example, new projects, ideas, or just sitting. 'The utility of the vase,' said the Chinese philosopher Lao Tsu, 'is in what is not there.' That is to say that the value of the container is the space it has for what goes in it. If it were solid it would not be a container. Like the vase, if we don't create the space and hold that space as important in itself, then we possibly miss out on the potential that the space provides us, even when we don't yet know exactly what to put in it.

Autumn is an opportunity to experience the concept of spaciousness in a different way. A tree that has lost its leaves shows us the bare and beautiful skeleton of its branch network. We can see further and wider with the absence of foliage. This too has a beauty to it.

In Eastern tradition, Autumn links to everything that is unknown. It can feel like a place that is empty rather than full. The harvest is over. The leaves, though beautiful in their turning, cannot be stopped from falling. The 'juice' for the year is beginning to wane and change. Activity is slowing down and stopping. We may feel unable to name exactly what this is for us but we can sense it.

For some people, and organisations, the push is to go into hyperactivity up to Christmas. This over-doing often leads to colds, exhaustion and burnout if it goes too far for too long. This doesn't mean that activity isn't a good thing, or that the activity has to stop. Overall, it is about noticing, being aware and curious so that you can attend to it with compassion, care and a plan to work with what is arising in a nurturing and supportive way. The gardener at this time of year knows which plants must be wrapped up for Winter and which are happy to remain in-situ but there is always the surveillance of intentional attention to what is needed in the moment.

Here is an exercise for using the time when Autumn's harvest has been gathered in, we conserve and preserve the fruits and crops we want, and have begun to consider the pruning to be done later in November.

Sorting the 'wheat from the chaff' exercise

Find a space where you won't be disturbed for half an hour. Have some pens (maybe in a couple of different colours) and your journal handy.

Close your eyes and take a few deeper than normal in-breaths and very slow, a little bit longer, out-breaths so that you can let whatever you were doing before this exercise be put aside and you can arrive fully here in this moment.

Imagine yourself in a tiny village in the middle of the countryside. You have never been here before but somehow it all looks and feels familiar and welcoming. The street beneath your feet is cobbled and the village feels very old indeed. Either side of you are higgledy-piggledy narrow streets leading from where you are as you walk down the central main street of the village. You can just about see some iron gates at the very end and what looks like a green and beautiful garden.

Take a few minutes to get a sense of what is around you in this street. Pause.

As you begin to walk slowly up this cobbled street you notice that to either side of you, the shops are named after the months of the year. To your left is January, to the right February, a little further on is March to your left and April to your right. Each shop frontage is of a different colour. In the shop windows and inside the shop are your memories of that particular month. Only you can see them. In January you see what things you did, accomplished, noticed, read or felt in that month. Take some time to visit the January window display and shop. There is a basket there for you to take whatever memories you wish to gather on your walk down this street, known as **This Year in the Village of Memory Lane**.

Here are three questions to guide you:

- What has meant the most to you in this month? Brought you joy? Learning?
- What are you grateful for in this month?
- What would be best to leave behind as no longer needed, at least for now?

When you are ready, move from January's shop to each succeeding month, taking your basket into each shop and asking the same questions.

When you have arrived at the end of this street and have explored all the months up to the present moment and you have what you need in your basket, you will find yourself in front of a beautiful wrought iron gate to a garden.

The garden is in the midst of harvest time and you are welcome to enter. This is your garden too. You open the gate and step onto soft grass with a gravel path. Put your basket down and take some minutes to visit this garden as it prepares for harvest. As the head gardener of your garden, you decide what stays and what goes. You are separating the wheat from the chaff from the land and gardens.

Review what you most want to preserve from the last nine or ten months of all the memories and experiences you have gathered.

- What gifts will you conserve and honour going forward?
- What needs to be pruned away to allow for new growth?
- What will you seed for the Spring?

Take some time to explore this as you wander in the garden.

When you feel that you have harvested what you need to and let go of what you must, thank yourself and the garden for the welcome you have had and the riches of this harvest and leave the garden, closing the gate behind you.

Make your way back down the cobbled central street until you reach the edge of the village and the place where you began this exploration.

When you are ready, open your eyes, and take a little time to capture what is essential in your journal. You might like to use one colour pen to indicate the 'harvest crop', a different colour for 'lesson learned' and a third for what must be 'let go of'.

This exercise could be revisited in the next season. Later in this chapter, I share some Autumn walks that can help explore your thinking further.

> ### Greenhousing moment
> When life has been tough, what kept you going when times were hardest? How does your 'metal' show up in the life you lead today? Has it changed over time?

Cultivating the quality of Grit

A cardinal quality of Autumn energy is **Grit**. Knowing what we stand for as a person and being in touch with our strengths under fire are important. Grit is what helps us to persevere when the chips are down or the pressure is high. We may need to be flexible and bend with the wind as trees do in Autumn, but still we stay grounded and courageous and persevere when challenges rise. We may not have the sun to warm our backs or the strong light of day as the days grow shorter, but we can have the capacity to know what we need to hold onto and stay in the game. Grit helps us do this.

"Reflection is the bridge between information and wisdom"

Michael Carroll

Autumn practices

Every season invites practices that are particularly resonant to that season and are relevant to the garden of our life. They help bring balance by engaging us in a way that acknowledges the character of the season, offering a way to pause and connect with what is around us as the season evolves and the weeks pass. Like Nature's wise apothecary, it is there to support us in our flourishing, one season at a time.

Journaling

Journaling is a reflective practice with many benefits. Autumn is a good time to begin if you have not done so before. You can journal about anything and everything, for any amount of time. Capturing even fleeting inner conversations can give shelter to the nuances and facets of your own emergent insights and wisdom. A year from now will give you a good point at which to review your progress.

This Autumn, begin a gratitude journal. Each evening before turning off the light to go to sleep, write down three things that you were grateful for in the course of the day. At the end of the month, look back to see if any patterns emerged that had been important for you. Keep this going for the whole of Autumn.

Other options:

Write about a tough challenge you tackled this year that you resolved and what you did to achieve that.

Journal about a conflict that is not yet resolved or an old issue within yourself that keeps nagging at you, although the situation itself may have long since passed. Make a promise to yourself to resolve it or to let it go. Finding a way to symbolically let it go can help too.

Journal about truthfulness and what it means to you.

When are you the most and least truthful with yourself or others? What has not been clear and needs to be? What activities are you engaged in that have become clouded with different variations on what is really happening or needs to happen? Where do you need to step forward, or back?

Clearing out, de-cluttering

Go through your cupboard, shed, or garage – anywhere that is cluttered or over-full – and collect what can go to a charity shop or be given away to others who might need it. Even if it is only a shelf or drawer, use the notion of pruning as a way to create more spaciousness and refining down to what is still in regular use, important to you, and gives you joy.

Take time to finish projects that have come to a halt or that you need to let go of. Unfinished half-done projects are great stress makers, calling to us way after they may no longer be as important as they were at one time. This could include broken kettles in a bag at the back of cupboard; broken zips in trousers unworn for two years because they're too small; the spices that sit in your cupboard half-used, bought years ago.

As in early Spring, Autumn is a good time to cleanse the body. Give your body respite and get rid of toxins from your diet. Consider a day of juice fasting if all other aspects of your health will allow you to do this.

Slowing down – Autumn energy is moving downward to nourish roots

The benefits of taking regular exercise are well-established. In Autumn consider including more practices like T'ai chi, yoga or Pilates where the energy is focussed on the breath.

Say 'thank you' in person

Call a friend who has been there for you when you most needed them, even if it was a long time ago. Tell that person what they did in just being themselves that was important to you. One way is to write them a letter, but instead of sending it, read it out loud to them. It might feel awkward or uncomfortable but you will both live through that. The importance here is voicing it from the heart face-to-face.

Getting closure

There may be conversations around you that are long overdue, relationships that are hanging by a thread and need your attention, or for you to make peace with the other person, or yourself. There may be some goodbyes to say, even if the person is no longer contactable. Find a ritual, or a cleansing process, like writing a letter to the person that you do not actually send; but the act of writing gives you space to clarify for yourself what you feel and need to say. When you have said all that needs to be said, consider burning it as a way to let it go.

Make a centrepiece or a table decoration with the bounty of Autumn

Collect things like colourful mini-pumpkins and squashes, curly hazel and dried flowers and harlequin corn cobs in straw baskets as an offering of seasonal colour.

Think fragrance

It is a good time to think about enhancing your home with the fragrances that you love most and that as you breathe them in, bring a smile to your face. Perhaps a mixture or a single signature note for the season. If you are not sure, test samples in stores.

Contemplate 'lagrom'

Lagrom is a Swedish term that means happiness can be found in contentment with simply being in the now. Journal about what 'lagrom' would look like in your life.

You shall ask
What use are dead leaves?
and I will tell you
They nourish the sore earth
You shall ask
What reason is there for winter?
And I will tell you
To being about new leaves
You shall ask

Why are the leaves so green?
And I will tell you
Because they are rich with life
You shall ask
Why must summer end?
And I will tell to
So that the leaves can die

by Nancy Wood (1974)
from *Many Winters.* Courtesy of the Nancy Wood Literary Trust.

Postcard from the Autumn Hedgerow

THIS SPACE FOR WRITING MESSAGES

Post Card

FOR ADDRESS ONLY

PLACE STAMP HERE

DOMESTIC ONE CENT

FOREIGN TWO CENTS

Preparing for your weekly seasonal walks

1. First start by finding a place to sit or be at rest.

Take a few moments to get a sense of where you are. Become aware of where you are sitting or standing. Your feet should be flat on the ground, with your body balanced evenly between both feet. Shoulders are relaxed back and down and your spine erect but not rigid. Have your knees ever so slightly bent. If you are sitting have both feet flat on the ground, arms relaxed, perhaps in your lap. You may wish to drop your gaze down to the ground to remove any distractions or close your eyes if it feels comfortable for you to do so where you are.

Bring your attention to your breath and notice where you feel your in and out breathing most distinctly. It could be your abdomen, your chest, or the sensation of cool air flowing in and out of your nostrils. Follow the pace of your breath in and out without changing anything, just following it as it flows naturally for a few moments, perhaps a minute or two. Allow your body to release any tension.

When you are centred in yourself, reconnect with your body as it sits or stands where it is. Feel the holding solidness of the ground beneath your feet or the firmness of the chair or bench where you sit.

2. Consider your intention for your walk today.

You might choose a word or a quality or use one of the questions below as a walking prompt. If you do then let the question rest lightly as you walk, allowing whatever arrives in your head and heart to be. You can use the same questions over many weeks or choose a different one. You may notice different experiences presenting.

3. Use all of your senses.

When you are ready, begin your walk by holding openness to the qualities of the season in mind. Allow yourself to tune into what you can see, hear and sense on your walk – almost perhaps as if you were seeing it for the first time.

Over the next weeks and months of the season pay close attention to newness as you walk, increasing your range of noticing what is new and fresh in you or in Nature, the parks and gardens around you as the season shifts day by day and week by week.

Try to bring a childlike sense of curiosity and joyful wonder, as if you were seeing things for the very first time. Slow down your speed and upgrade your attention to what is all around you. Really notice the detail as you walk. Give yourself time to be fascinated, whether it is by the intricacies of a gossamer web, the colours and patterns in a leaf, or the bark of a tree. The choice is yours!

4. Give yourself a few uninterrupted moments to really look at something from every angle.

See it as if you had never seen one of its kind before in your life. Sniff it, touch it gently. Turn it over if you can. Close your eyes for a moment with it resting in your hand or on your finger. Think about its journey up to now and how it may have come into existence. Take in the nuance of its shade or colour, texture, line, and position.

5. Capture the essence at the finish for your Season's diary.

Use your *Postcard from the Hedgerow* to capture some words or a quick sketch, whatever suits you, that most helpfully summarises your walk. These cards, as the weeks go by, will be part of your weekly bite-size journaling. It could be a phrase, a few sentences, a poem or a photo you took that most inspired you. You can make a copy of the postcard above or create your own. They capture a moment in time and are added to your collection as you travel through the year. Of course you may also want to write more but if you are new to journal writing this is a wonderful place to start because the space does not demand so much and they are very easy to carry with you anywhere.

Begin an album to hold them all or put them in your journal to look back on next Autumn.

6. Plant your intentions.

Consider your intention for your walk today. You might choose 'awareness', or a colour, or a feeling like 'peace' or 'curiosity'. Or you might choose to use one of the questions below as a walking prompt. If you do, then let the question rest lightly as you walk allowing whatever arrives in your head and heart to be. You can use the same questions over many weeks or choose a different one. You may notice different experiences presenting themselves each time.

Autumn walks

Use these prompts as a loose guide when you're walking, or simply commit to a weekly outdoor date with yourself. Each walk will take you either through the streets where you live, or to a park or garden you have chosen.

Some questions to ponder on your Autumn walks

What do you need to let go of in your work or your life? What is no longer necessary or useful? Where do you need to make more space? Perhaps there is some thinking, an attitude or a situation that you have outgrown?

What do you need to do in order to consider allowing something new to germinate for next Spring?

Find a tree that you really like that still has its leaves, and take some time to really look at the colours and structure of an individual leaf as it is turning from green to rust to brown. Know that as it does, the tree's sap is moving down into the roots of the tree, where in Spring it will rise again to bring fresh green buds on bare branches. If this tree has a message for you, or a metaphor, about where you are right now in your life, what would it be?

Walk with the word 'gratitude' in mind and see what arises in you. As you walk, try to think of at least ten things that you are grateful for having done, seen or experienced so far this season or this year.

Reviewing in threes: what three things stand out as the best for you this past year? What three things would you like more of next year? What three things have brought a life lesson with them?

On your walk, find one aspect of Nature around you that encapsulates what Autumn means for you and take a photo of it. Write about it in your journal.

A circular seasonal diagram divided into segments:

WINTER
- Seeking depth & inspiration: the mystery of the not known & the spirit of life
- Letting be: stilling the mind
- REFLECTION
- FEAR
- GRACE
- WATER / W

SPRING
- Directing energy upwards towards growth
- Setting clear goals
- Creating possibilities
- DYNAMISM
- ANGER
- BLOSSOM
- WOOD / W

SUMMER
- Maturing and ripening of endeavours: heartfelt communication, passion & flow
- Relationships in work or play
- JOY
- SADNESS
- FLOURISH
- FIRE / F

LATE SUMMER
- Nurturing & preserving the abundance: the grounding to stay centred
- Appreciating the bounty
- SUPPORT
- WORRY
- HARVEST
- EARTH / E

AUTUMN
- Honouring integrity at root level
- Honouring with humility, precision & clarity
- Pruning and clarifying
- LETTING GO
- LOSS
- GRATITUDE
- METAL / M

a) the elemental metaphor
b) essence
c) when there is imbalance
d) a gift
e) a practice
f) an intention

© Karyn Prentice
Design: Kelly Alderdice,
2Ten Graphic Design

PART 2
through the gardening lens

CHAPTER 7

introduction:
why use the garden as a
metaphor for life?

"Each day calls us to tend life beyond ourselves"

Tom Balles

Surveying your landscape: the garden of your life

Nature speaks a universal language that can be understood by people all over the world.

To begin, we will explore how the language of good gardening can be used to guide you in making your own life flourish.

As a metaphor for life design, the language of gardening is rich in images, words and ideas to help you design and shape the life you want. It can help you appreciate anew the garden you currently have, and in this section of the book, you will be encouraged to take a fresh look at your own garden as it unfolds through the seasons.

A garden, like a life, has its own rhythm and tempo. For example, regular weeding little and often beats three hours of intense hard work.

Over the course of this book we cover a 12-month cycle, and, of course, as in Nature, each cycle repeats. Yet no garden remains exactly the same from one year to the next.

The word *palingenesis* refers to the intrinsic ability of life to regenerate itself and to give birth to new life over and over again. Immortality, at least so far, is not an option but we can look at how mini-cycles within cycles can inform us in order to help us make better choices each time around, whenever we can. In Nature we see the rolling cycle of the seasons over a year and, at the same time, some plants, like trees, take much longer than a year to achieve their full growth. Nature is a teacher we can learn from, be inspired by and allow to refresh and resource us. As Tom Balles writes in his book *Dancing The Ten Thousand Things*, 'Nature is a part of us. What takes place outside also takes place inside!'[16]

Our garden may be available to us 24 hours a day, seven days a week, but gardens also need time to rest. Rotating crops, and land laying fallow support the true tending of the land. The metaphor of the garden reminds us of the importance of balance, and the consequences to us of imbalance.

In my experience, good gardeners are humble, hugely skilful and very pragmatic. They build what they know from hands-on experience and by trial and error, most of the time. They are happy to share what they know with other gardeners, swap seeds, tips, and certainly stories. When something doesn't work they learn from it and make adjustments. There is nothing that gives a gardener greater satisfaction than getting the garden in shape for the season, even if sometimes that is back-breaking digging in a wet and muddy allotment.

Gardeners encourage and enable plants to flourish. They help to create optimum conditions for the plant to fulfil its potential. While the plants have to do the growing themselves, usually at their own pace, the gardener has an understanding of the whole environment, much more than the individual plant can have. Gardeners bring their wisdom to bear in considering what and where to plant and tend. They must be patient, creative, hardy, flexible, thick-skinned and sensitive to nuances of change very quickly. They can't tell their plants what to do, but they can create an optimum environment so the plant can get on with its work of growing and flourishing. In effect, gardeners are natural life coaches.

We can learn a lot by following their example and think of our everyday life in terms of a garden, to carry out the same tending and befriending towards ourselves, and to restore and nourish ourselves as we harvest a crop of successes, however we choose to define these.

Most of us find ourselves playing many other roles besides being the gardeners of our own lives. We may be fixers, enablers, supporters, cheerleaders, carers, employees, companions, parents and partners, helping others to thrive.

When I was a kid, I learned the phrase 'cobbler's shoes' which meant, as far as I understood it, that the cobbler mends everyone else's shoes and his own fall into poor condition because they come last. We need to not come last in our own estimation, consideration and care. Our gardens – whether they are tiny window boxes or acres of land – matter. *You* matter.

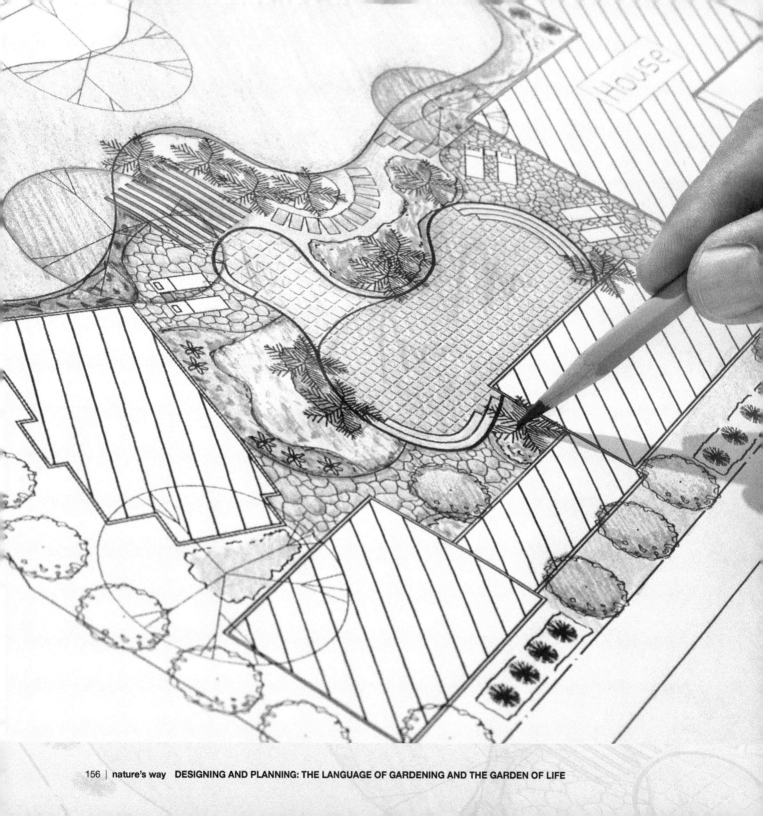

CHAPTER 8

designing and planning: the language of gardening and the garden of life

Planning and designing your life garden

Every garden requires loving attention to both the overall concept and the 'down-in-the-detail' care of each plant and the space it inhabits. Whether your garden is a window box or stretches over many acres, size is not of itself the most important thing. A small space can give great pleasure.

If you are content with the life you have right now, this may mean little change is required in your garden. That is great.

On the other hand, you may wish to re-design some small aspects of your garden while leaving important, long-established things where they are. This means looking at what can, or might be, different, and creating a plan.

This may be the time for you to really think about what your life garden needs, and an opportunity for you to play with some new ideas. These are just some ways to approach thinking about the garden of your life. After all, this is about evolving the environment around you that will support you in the ways you want to live your life.

Borders

Borders in garden design can offer many exciting variations in design. They act as a boundary between one part of the garden and another. Borders can frame an aspect of a garden and be in themselves a cornucopia of colour, texture and size. They can be quiet, sturdy and evergreen; be easy to manage or a lot of work.

Without good borders and consideration of what can encroach and what is welcome in an outdoor garden, some plants can be invasive and deprive other plants of light and nutrients. Others can be 'companion plants' where each benefits from the presence of the other.

The borders and boundaries in the garden of life are equally interesting. They can represent the place where exciting things happen. At the edges of our experience, where comfort meets bravery, it may be a place for us to dare a bit more. Sometimes we can be very aware of that spot and shy away from going further, bigger, deeper.

Most of us have borders between what we do with ease and what would be a stretch or even a huge challenge. This is known as our 'learning edge' or 'stretch zone'. When planning the garden of the life we want, exploring the boundaries and border lands of what we have and what we would like gives us the opportunity to redefine our boundaries and seed them with enthusiasm and creativity. Some boundaries and borders will be internal ones about our confidence, and the stories we tell ourselves about what we think is possible and what is not.

In designing your garden, consider what you might experiment with that you could introduce briefly into the garden, like an annual summer plant bringing a burst of colour.

…Or something that could add some necessary structure that can offer solid intention of something to bring into your life over the longer term.

…Or something that may grow slowly, flower regularly and develop over time…

Where do you need colour, structure, and interest to frame the main parts of your life?

What can you plant that will have room to flourish?

Imagining

Find some space where you won't be disturbed and where you feel really at ease. Have some paper nearby, or your journal, to capture what arises. You are going to spend some time dreaming and imagining your ideal life garden.

Close your eyes and imagine... if your life was a garden, how would you describe it? What would be in it if you were standing on a balcony looking down onto it? What would you see? What would it look like, smell like, feel like, if you were right in the midst of it?

What elements are in your life right now that you treasure? What parts have become long established over many years?

Don't censor it or worry about what it all might mean. At this point you are just allowing your imagination to roam. Let yourself just notice what emerges for the moment, whether words, sentences, sketches; whatever arises is fine. You don't have to act on any aspect of this. If you often have a highly active, self-critical part of yourself ready to give you advice, then tell it to go get a coffee somewhere down the road and let you play here for a while.

My life garden

- What things are absolute musts in this garden?

- What is in your garden now that needs some kind of attention?

- What would you like to see in the garden that is not there now?

Inside this space insert the features of your life that cannot be moved because they are intrinsic to the overall design. You can represent these in shapes, colours, in any way that works for you.

What is the relative size of these elements in relationship to the overall size of your life garden? Think of how much they feature in your life right now. This may be in terms of the time they take up in an average week or month or longer, or the importance of the relationship, or the responsibility involved.

In an outdoor garden there may be a large, well-established tree with extensive root structures, or a pond. Where the house sits and its direction also usually cannot be changed. There may be long-established favourite activities in your life, i.e. garden plants that you want to remain in the places they are in now, even if they were moveable.

This will give you a sense of what space remains that is negotiable; space that you can work with to shape, change, clear or alter. Even if you end up with the tiniest of free space to play with, this can still be a place of creativity and opportunity.

There may be some bare spaces longing to be filled with new life. Or there may be a longing for more space to breathe. Perhaps space has arisen because something important has died away or has been lost. The shadow of that may still be there and it can be hard to come to terms with that kind of space when it is unwelcome. What does enough space look like in your ideal garden?

Designing your garden for life

Having imagined this ideal space, take your pens and paper and roughly sketch the shape for your ideal life garden.

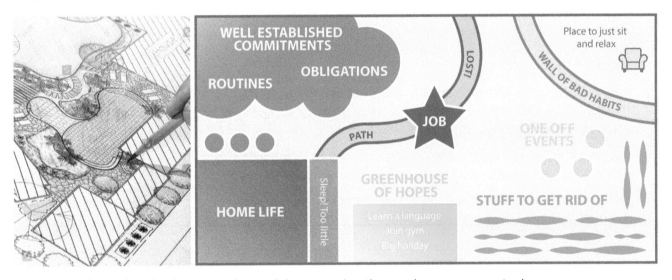

First, make a sketch of your garden as it is now using the garden as your metaphor, using any shape you like, as all gardens vary...

Then, draw a second one that represents your ideal design.

Borders – Well established elements that shape and contain your life. For example, your financial means, family and friends, spiritual or religious beliefs, values and principles.

Plants, trees, bushes – We all have 168 hours available to us a week. Consider the elements in your day-to-day life in an average week. With each thing you place in the garden, its size should mirror the amount of time and/or space it occupies. Think about your job, the hours you are asleep, chores, committed time to groups or others, activities that are regular fixtures, rest and recreation, hobbies, 'me' time. Put them all in your design.

Places to sit and rest

Vistas, features, places to resource yourself, potter and think

Spaces between what is there

Questions to reflect on for your ideal garden

- What could, with some time, skills and creativity, be moved or changed? Where is there some potential for movement, change, alteration, or what would benefit from a change of aspect, soil or light for it to flourish?

- Looking back over the last year, or more, what events began as a simple 'one-off' and have metaphorically self-seeded into many more activities or a bigger commitment that now, as you reflect, you might wish to re-design, in some way?

- Looking forward, are there some one-off activities or features that will come along in the next 12 months that you want to accommodate and make space for in your life garden?

- What has spilled over onto the path of everyday life that you want to keep and what would you prefer to cut away?

- Carving out space just to stop and stare is not merely fanciful. Is the space in your current garden design all work and no rest? Is it space in which to savour and appreciate? How can you include space for rest and renewal in your garden?

- Consider your current and future commitments, including relationships and where these fit in the design of your life.

- Where do you need more, or less, structure?

- Where do you feel most alive in your garden? What feels energetically heavy? What is just about surviving and what is thriving?

- Where do you need a new path, space, a special feature?

- What can you see from each corner? Can you appreciate particular vantage points?

- How do you move from one part of your life garden to another?

- Where is there space for deeply rooted, long-standing aspects of your life? By contrast, like annual summer plants, what is a burst of energy and colour, but short lived? Both add something valuable to the garden. Think of annuals like one-off projects; something short term, hopefully enjoyable or as necessary tasks.

- Where do you need more colour?

- Where do you need to make space for longer-term projects that yield fruit over time?

- What is growing but needs more light, or water, or nutrients?

- What is already in the garden exactly where it needs to be?

- What is in the garden but needs a new place, or to be pruned or dug up?

- What will help your life garden to flourish and what will hinder it? Use a gardener's eye to assess where judicious pruning will support new growth later on in the year.

- What aspects or projects have outgrown the place they occupy in your life? Or have crowded out other things that are also important but have not had enough of your time or attention?

- What might need divining into smaller chunks, delegated to others, given away, or just stopped?

- What would thrive better in another part of your garden, with different conditions today than when it was first begun?

And … what else?

"I have a room all to myself; it is nature"

Henry David Thoreau

CHAPTER 9
tools for tending and befriending

Tending and befriending the life garden

The metaphor of the garden is a rich one and some terms lend themselves both to the language of the garden *where you live*, be it window box, acreage or anything in between, and the garden that you *are*. As the naturalist John Muir said: 'When we try to pick out anything by itself, we find it hitched to everything else in the Universe.'

What does 'tending and befriending our life garden' mean?

- Building our capacity as a compassionate observer of our inner life, as we would observe and tend our external garden.

- Being really present to, and welcoming of, the nuances of change as they show up.

- Finding a way to be at ease with our own nature. A daffodil does not long to be a rose. Both are beautiful but different. This means not comparing ourselves to someone else, a surefire way to invite in negativity.

Remember that each turn of the season means change, and change is a part of life, our inner life as much as our outer one. To tend and befriend the life garden is to create the very best conditions we can for what we wish to see grow.

Tending tactics: getting down to the ground

Weeding

In any garden, if there is one activity that is as continual as the painting of the Forth Bridge, it is weeding. That means the job is a long one and by the time you finish it is time to start again from the beginning. The good news is, whereas once you start painting a bridge you must carry on and finish it, with weeding 'little and often' is the best approach.

Weeds can be the most vigorous, robust and persistent form of greenery. Though we can give love and attention to a beautiful plant, brought home from the nursery or garden centre, and lavish it with attention, it might still perish. The ordinary weed, even with no attention at all, thrives regardless.

In the garden of life, negative thoughts are like weeds. If we are not vigilant they can mount up and stymie our good intentions for change. Like garden weeds, they don't need much to keep them going and can take over. A few weeds we can live with, but when they become dominant in our thought pattern we need to attend to them so that we can see plans and projects take off and grow.

For example, you might wish to start a new hobby, or go to the gym more regularly or get up a half hour earlier for some pursuit of interest. It is very easy to begin the litany of 'Well, tomorrow is better because I will be at home that day…', or 'Until I clear a space in the house to put the craft materials there is no point…'; 'I am going to miss the third and eighth session so maybe I shouldn't start…'; 'I am too old, too young, too disorganised.' All of these may carry some truth, and these thoughts may also be the weeds that spring up abundantly that keep us from the intentions we had to begin with. Even the notion of getting rid of every weed, or every distraction or negative thought can be an example of all-or-nothing thinking. More weeds than ever! So beginning to see the wood for the trees, as the saying goes, is to start swathing a path to your destination, one tug at a weed at a time, one refusal to let the negative thought multiply.

So how is your balance of thinking? Are you biased more towards optimism and thinking positively? Or do you think that in order to be realistic you have to err on the side of pessimistic outcomes so as not to be disappointed? Or maybe you are somewhere in between? Positivity need not be 'Pollyanna-type' thinking that ignores reality in favour of a rose-tinted picture. However, without a good balance of positive thinking, hope and energy, then changes to the status quo are harder. Weeds and negative thoughts are persistent, so regular checking on the quality of your thinking is vital for your mental and emotional ecology.

Like all craftspeople, gardeners have the necessary tools of their trade for the different jobs they carry out in the garden. There are rakes, hoes, even a pick axe, for the really tough bits of rock or root, and hand tools like a dibber, a trowel, and fork. Each tool helps in differing situations.

Make a list of the tools you have that help you live your life. These may be small gadgets that lighten the load or support and help you on a daily basis. What things or processes really help you lead the life you do? What processes hamper you? What needs refurbishing, renewing, trashing or gifting to someone else?

Pricking out

This garden term describes the process of separating and lifting the tiny new shoots of growth from a seed tray of many such shoots and transplanting them to their own pot for the next stage of growing. If seeds have thrown up many shoots they will be too crowded together in the tray to thrive. Each plant doesn't get the benefit of enough space to grow to its potential. Carrots, for instance, or beetroot, if not thinned out, produce vegetables that are small and puny.

For ideas and projects, a strategy and a process for choosing and selecting are vital. We might say 'yes' to too many things, or people, and then have not enough time to devote to any of them in order for them to flourish. Over-commitment often leads to overwhelm and this is not helpful for a healthy life garden.

So think of 'pricking out' as choosing a process of review that works for you, that will support how you check on the viability of a project or plan so that you can nurture it and give it the right amount of room to grow. Saying 'no' is part of this process of being more selective. You may already know where there is too much going on in a small space of your life and, as a result, all of your energy can be compromised. At the end of the day some things planted, even with the best intentions, can fail despite years of experience, knowledge, the highest quality seeds and tools, plus all the best tips from Grandpa's gardening books. Sometimes this happens, after heroic effort and lots of time and money. A gardener takes stock of the learning gained from planting that particular plant, in that spot, at that time of the year, and makes some calculations about whether to try in that spot again or change an element of choice. A good gardener doesn't keep doing the same thing because he or she works out that they will get the same outcome and that is a waste of time, effort and plants. Gardeners are stoic, and persevere to the point of stubbornness. Gardeners are also patient. In the life garden, cultivating patience and being an agile learner are crucial.

Dig, dig, and dig

The traditional gardening advice is to dig before Winter is over so winter frost will freeze and break up heavy soil. All soils benefit from extra organic matter so spreading compost or manure on the surface and digging that in will improve any soil.

Looking after the soil is a big, ongoing job. It need not be onerous but it does require our constant attention. In the garden of your life circumstances can take us, even temporarily, into exhaustion, overwhelm or burnout. Like the land, we can become 'nutrition poor' and drained of all our juicy nature. We need to put some enrichment back into our own metaphorical garden because, under pressure, we demand so much more of ourselves. For example, building a resource library of reading that inspires you, or taking some time to visit and walk in public gardens contributes to the restoration of a sense of balance in their beauty and grace. For other folks, it may be to reconnect to a spiritual or religious practice that can bring sanctuary from the hurly-burly onslaught of the rest of the week's relentless requirements. Or just to sit quietly with no more to do than connect to the gratitude of what is already present, right in the moment.

This is like turning the soil of our soul. Gardeners know that soil sustains life, and the pressure of too many hours working or caring for others, or a combination of both, carries an intensity that needs the balance of focused self-care, support and attention in order for us to thrive. The small treasures in life become evident when we stop, take space and slow down

Dedicated spaces

The greenhouse

The greenhouse is the place we put tender young plants to protect them while they are beginning to grow. Plants that are more susceptible to the cold can be lovingly stored for the Winter in a heated greenhouse until the warmer weather allows them to be placed outdoors or planted into the ground. The weather in certain places can still be too harsh, even in early Spring, if there is the potential of frost. Here, under the cover of glass, the extra warmth of the glass walls and the sunlight allow them to survive. Seeds, in a tray of good soil, can become strong. Small, vulnerable and young plants can be protected while they grow.

We can do the same with new ideas or projects that are in an embryonic state. A potential new idea, exposed too soon to commentary, criticism or nay-sayers, can be killed before you have had time to explore it yourself and determine if it is viable. 'Greenhousing'[17] is a term used by creative people that describes putting a nascent idea somewhere safe while you go about:

- Gathering information
- Checking sources and conducting research
- Identifying your needs, resources, finances or support
- Getting input and wider perspectives

It means you are able to acknowledge your idea, but recognise it as still being in the tender phases of creation. Perhaps you have several of these infant ideas and you have yet to decide which could fly, given more of your time and attention. The greenhouse is the place to put them, even temporarily, while you do what you need to do without losing sight of your initial enthusiasm, energy and intention. It doesn't mean that seeking out perspectives that challenge you isn't good. It is all about timing. Sometimes, even with our best interests in mind, others can tell you first all the reasons why something won't work before you have even had a chance to find out if it would be viable. We can lose courage before we have even begun. The greenhouse is a staging post along the way of creative exploration.

Thinking shed

My husband has a shed in the garden. It is full of what I call 'toot' and he calls 'very important things'. Old tools, a dead kettle, a rug from the kitchen I thought I threw out ten years ago. Sometimes he goes in there and just stands looking at stuff. He tells me that as he looks around, a solution to a problem he is having with the garden suddenly comes to him, or he spots just the tool he needs for a particular job, one that he had forgotten he had. Almost every time.

I like to call my shed 'the thunder box'. My colleague calls hers a 'reflection studio'. You might think of your space as a thinking shed, or play room, or some other name that conjures up a place, removed from the everyday, that allows you to access more of the extraordinary.

For me, it is where I go to see what flows into my mind. I use a room in my house – not my office, where the desk and computer live – but another room that contains most of my books and a futon that can double as a bed. I take a pad and a pot of coloured pens, and a cup of coffee or tea, and I sit. It might be for 15 minutes or a half hour. It gives me respite from all the other jobs around the house, the screams of emails demanding attention or my demanding mind that says, 'find an answer!'

I also use a couple of cafés that offer this same kind of space. The bustle, noise and comings-and-goings of others works for me to create a personal space bubble and I can do some 'thunder box' work over a coffee.

So quiet or noisy might work for you, or a combination of the two. It might be space in your home, office, or a garden studio, to give ideas a little space, metaphorically, and to rest for the moment.

"Sanctuary is a place where a person is at home with his own company. It is a place of rest, a powerful pause"

Terry Hershey, The Power of Pause

Potting shed

This is different from your thinking space. This is where you cut, paste, stick, colour, write, get messy and store the tools that will support you in the reflection, experimentation and discovery of what you want to grow in the garden of your life, and how you best want to tend and encourage to flourish what is already there.

For instance you might want some of these items:

- A computer or access to one
- Plenty of white and coloured paper: A1, A3 or A4
- Lots of coloured felt tips or other writing and drawing instruments
- Your journal
- Index cards, scissors
- Files and folders and an accessible storage system

Playing with coloured pens

When I first bought a brand new set of some 30 colours of good quality felt tip coloured pens and stood them up in an old but pretty mug, I had it on my desk in front of my computer for quite some time before I gave myself permission to use them as part of my thinking process. I finally let myself go beyond the self-inhibiting thought:'I am not an artist', to use them during phone calls with clients to highlight things as they arose in conversation or to add a flourish in a different colour as I mind mapped my way through my own projects.

A mind map[18] is a diagram that helps us get ideas and information down on paper by arranging them around a central topic or idea you want to explore and then radiating outwards, creating a kind of web of ideas in a free-flowing creative way of capturing related thoughts as they arise. Usually different colours are used for different ideas to make it more memorable and stimulating for the brain.

A mind map can be a quick way to capture ideas as they arrive in the mind without the constraint of organising them into any specific linear order while you are thinking. Beginning with a central idea in a circle in the middle of a page of blank paper, even a single word, like 'me', is fine. Turn the paper so it is wider than it is taller to give you more room so you can then draw four or five 'spokes' that lead from the centre circle you drew out to the edge of the page. Use different colours for each spoke. Give each of these 'spokes' a name, like 'easy things to do', 'things to eliminate', 'skills', and so on. Then for five minutes write what arises under, or beside, each spoke. You don't need sentences, just key words that will remind of you of the thought you had when you wrote it down. For example, 'more walks' might give a sense of what you know you mean without the extra words to give you a picture in your mind. Continue to populate your map with words or even little marks or symbols. Then leave your mind map to incubate for at least a day or two before you pick it up and work on it for a further five minutes. Three or four rounds like this and you will build your map. For more ideas about mind mapping, see Recommended Reading on page 242 in Chapter 11.

There is something exhilarating about letting yourself use coloured pens or pencils for no other reason than pleasure. As a child, I would bring home drawings I had made at school during the day. I don't think I have ever met a small child who, on arriving home with a drawing, said to mother, father or care-giving adult: 'Well, I did this at school this morning but, frankly, I am not satisfied with the colour, the angle, or the perspective. I think it compares poorly with the other children's work and I am seriously considering at my age (7 years old) to give up colouring as pointless.' No, we don't hear kids say that. They say: 'Look what I did at school today!'

In my work with adults, where I might invite them to draw something that came up for them, I often hear them disparage their attempts, even when they are pretty good. So often we lose the free flow of just enjoying using colours to make a mark, or a doodle, without feeling unless we are officially designated 'artists', our efforts are not worthwhile.

Create a book of 'likes'

Start with a journal of blank or lined pages, or both, according to your preference. You can create your own from plain or lined paper and hole-punch the pages ready to put in a binder.

In this you will be collecting things that attract or interest you: pictures, places, images, ideas, even if you don't do anything specific with them. At this stage, there is no triage process; just whatever takes your fancy. These are your seed supplies. Collect as much and as many as you wish.

You can use **Pinterest** as a digital form of gathering, or other ways to collect your findings. It is up to you. I have a personal preference for the kinaesthetic approach of being able to turn, touch, and handle paper. You choose. People are coming back to paper as a way to capture their ideas. You can do this with index cards too, creating a card for each idea. Be playful and peruse your stationery outlets and shops near you and find what appeals most. This 'book of likes' is your **seed catalogue** of what you might decide to grow. A place to come back to, again and again, to what attracts you. There may be a theme among the items you collect. You might consider it for a certain space in your life garden? What is important, and of the moment, will also influence what you like and choose. Some things will be familiar likes to you, perhaps you have always liked a certain place to go to, or longed for a change in a certain aspect of your life. There may be one or two things there that you want to incarnate in the refreshed design of your life garden.

Give yourself time to do this and don't set an end date. Take a little time now and again to look back and check on what you have collected, asking these questions, or ones that work best for you:

- What makes your heart sing?
- What brings a smile, or energy, to you when you see an item in your catalogue?
- What does it mean to thrive in your garden of life?
- What seeds of newness feel important right now?
- What is already in the garden that just needs some refreshing?

Soil

The quality and constituency of soil in a garden is critically important in gardening. It will impact on your choices of plants. An outdoor gardener takes care of the soil in a number of ways. He might have to enrich the soil to help chosen plants survive and thrive. The soil is turned, aerated, fed. Adding mulch or compost at certain times of the year supports the chemistry of the earth, the worms that live in it and the seeds and roots of the plant. So much of the process of growing happens underground before we even see that brave stalk poking its head out of the earth. Getting the right amount of water, not too much and not too little, is also important.

In the life garden your soil is the core amalgamation of your experiences, your ancestry and everything you have learned along the way, including your values and beliefs, education, and culture. What happened to you last year, ten years ago or a generation ago may still be influencing who you are today. Getting to know yourself and the driving forces that take you towards one choice and away from others is all influenced by the experiences, filters, concerns, values and stories we have told ourselves throughout our lives or were experienced by you in your family of origin.

Your metaphorical soil can change over time, can be richer in nutrients and have what it needs to flourish, or it can become impoverished when we have not given it the right nourishment, rest and support. This can change over time so it is vital to test the condition of your life garden soil so that you can decide what it needs in order to receive the new seeds and plants of the future. For whatever you wish to make happen in your life, attention to who you are in your core is part of that process.

Roots

The roots system of a plant is its lifeline. Trees, for instance, have a taproot, which brings water up to the branches and leaves. It has other roots that bring nutrition up through the trunk. When we look at a large tree with a wide span of branches we can count on there being roots that go wider and deeper than the part of the tree that is visible.

When I was a kid, our family used to go and picnic in Griffith Park, which was up in the hills above Los Angeles. There was a wooded area covered in ferns and huge trees. We played around the base of the trunks. Lots of trees there had roots that bulged up out of the ground like knobbly brown crusty knees. The earth piled up around these bulges so that we could walk on them, almost like a separate raised path, without having to step off on to the ground itself. We came to know a number of these old trees. We knew them by their markings: a large gap; maybe a scar made over time and by Nature; a place where a certain bark pattern seemed to show a face in its design. If they had been perfectly smooth with no scars it would have been harder to know them. We didn't think the markings made them ugly. We thought they made each tree unique. We used to make up stories about how the tree got its markings, almost as if it had been a rite of passage.

We all have roots too. And plenty of stories about how we came to be where we are in our life. We are all survivors of whatever has happened to us so far. As long as you are holding this book right now, count yourself a survivor of life. As the writer Flannery O'Connor said: 'Anybody who survived his childhood has enough information to last him the rest of his days'.[19]

There may be some things in your garden with deep roots connecting you to your childhood, and beyond that to your family ancestry, and beyond that to the elders of many generations. In small and large ways they contribute to who you are today even when those roots, like those of a tree, are not always visible.

The uprooted has been used to describe what happens to us when we are, due to circumstances sometimes not of our making, uprooted. It is not a simple process and it can be a painful one too for many reasons. It can mean being taken abruptly from all that we know and care about. But it is a serious one, even when the outcomes are positive and wished for. In all cases, great care is needed to look after what is taken from the soil to its new place of planting. Anyone who has planted a new tree in their garden knows that certain times of the year are better than others for replanting to ensure the tree will thrive in its new position. Special caretaking of a tree with its bare roots exposed is important, as it is for us humans.

Sometimes a smaller plant than a tree has outgrown its container. We say the plant in question has become 'pot-bound'. This means that the plant is too big for the container it is in and its roots can't get any nutrients, or spread themselves to any new earth. This can be true for humans too. We can have grown too large for the life we are living, or the life we are living needs more space for it to continue to grow and flourish.

The condition of the root ball must be tended to so that when any new action takes place the plant has the best start in its new home.

When you think of your own roots, how does this metaphor speak to you?

Let's look at a few exercises that can help you gather and review more knowledge about you and your roots.

What looked like a good spot to begin with is not seeing the plant through the turn of the seasons and it would do better by being moved, or even divided into several smaller thriving plants.

In terms of life's garden, for any changes you might want to make it is important to first consider your root system, which includes your background, values, elders and ancestors' stories that have contributed to who you are today. This includes the things that have positively nourished your root system, and those elements that may have been thwarting your progress at some stage but you have found ways to adapt and change and become more of who you are.

What aspects of your life have the longest, richest root system and continue to sustain you today?

What's *your* 'taproot'? The central dominant root that has been a mainstay in your early growth and development?

Tracking your root system

Take a large sheet of plain white paper, or an old roll of wallpaper that you can use the blank side for also works well for this exercise. If not, construct your own by taping together smaller sheets of blank paper.

Draw a horizontal line about halfway down the page from the left edge of the paper across to the right hand side of the sheet edge. This line bisects the paper into two halves, half above the line and half below the line.

The left hand edge begins with the year of your birth. The right hand edge is the current year. You will be moving from left to right as you move through the key events in your life. So the older you are, the more space you will need on the right hand side of the paper.

You will be reflecting on your life in chunks, perhaps in decades, or five-year sections.

You can decide how much information to include here. The key is to capture the essence of the event and a date if you can, or at least the year of the event.

Give yourself time to do this activity at your leisure. Do this exercise over a week at least. Take time to just let the notion of recollection be at the back of your mind.

Above the line, use one colour ink and record key events that were good for you: successes, high points, great memories, happy times and the people who mattered most to you.

Below the line, using another colour moving from left to right chronologically, note down here times of great sadness, moments of loss, times when things did not work out. You don't need to dwell on these but noting them down is an act of honouring your journey. And the journey does not continue without leaving its marks and scars on us, just like those on a tree. They contribute to who we are today and the choices that we have made so far. They may influence the choices we make in the future. Allow yourself time to respect these moments too.

When you feel you have captured all the information possible, take some time to look over your whole root system, albeit a horizontal, rather than vertical, one. It is always, always impressive.

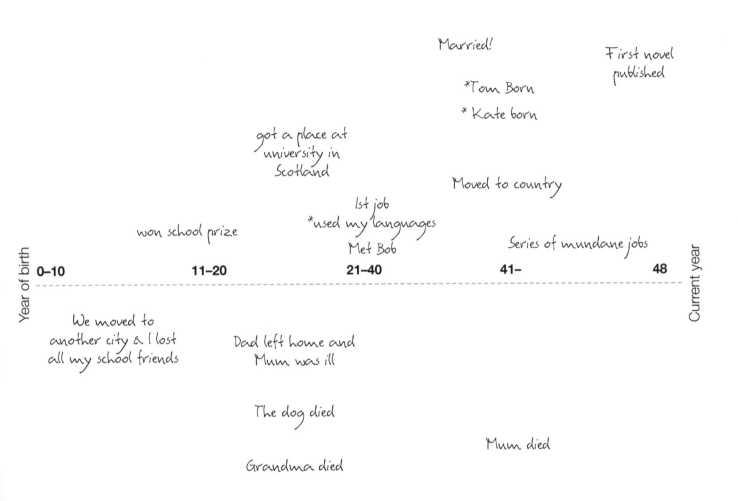

Married!

First novel
published

*Tom Born

* Kate born

got a place at
university in
Scotland

Moved to country

1st job
*used my languages
Met Bob

won school prize

Series of mundane jobs

Year of birth

0–10   11–20   21–40   41–   48

Current year

We moved to
another city & I lost
all my school friends

Dad left home and
Mum was ill

The dog died

Mum died

Grandma died

Here are some questions to reflect on:

- Where are the highest high points and the lowest low points? What correlation between these, if any, do you notice?

- Where do you owe yourself a pat on the back or more compassion than you may have already accorded yourself?

- What lessons have you learned from both the highs and the lows?

- What would you like to say to your younger self, with the benefit of hindsight?

- What wisdom can you offer your future self? What is wise, insightful, and helpful?

- What has helped you through the toughest times?

- In what ways have your experiences shaped your life to date?

- What strengths would others say you showed in the best/toughest of times?

- Do you see themes or patterns in your life?

- What does success mean to you in your life today?

Ancestors and elders

Some people are very lucky and can trace their families back many centuries. That wasn't the case for me. I had a very small family who all died, leaving no other relatives to draw upon as I became old enough to ask the hundreds of questions that will forever remain unanswered.

While I was blessed with supportive folks around me, I also had to invent my own imaginary 'back up' team. That gave me leave to pick and choose from historical and mythic figures, people that I knew and loved, and others that I admired and looked up to for qualities like courage, patience and grit. Two of those people, real folks, are still alive today and have been of inestimable support to me to this day.

Being grateful

If you have a good sense of your family tree, take some time to think about the kinds of issues each generation before you dealt with. What did they have to face with the resources they had at the time? Are there any patterns occurring over generations?

Even if you don't know how they fared, consider their time in an historical context.

Compose a letter to one or more of them thanking them for the characteristics and qualities that you most appreciate they have passed down to you and that you are holding on to as part of your root system. Acknowledge what might have been tough for them and what they may have coped with at the time. You may not be able to send it to them all this time later, but acknowledging them also acknowledges your recognition of your elder history.

Creating a board of elders

We can't time travel back to the past, more's the pity, perhaps. However, we can use the wonderful vehicle of our imagination to help us when we need to draw upon the past in order to enrich the future.

Close your eyes and take a few moments to relax into the chair you are sitting in. Follow your breath as it comes in and goes out. Be aware of your back, straight and upright in the chair, the sense of your legs against the substance of the chair and your feet flat on the floor, hands resting at ease in your lap. Follow a single breath as it comes in and flows out a few more times.

I invite you to picture a large wooden banqueting table or a stunning board room table of beautiful wood, lovingly made and burnished to an glorious shine. Around it are about eight to ten chairs made of the same beautiful wood. Over the next few minutes, taking the time that you need, you will be populating this table with people that have a quality, skill, talent or perspective that you would like to draw upon when making decisions. They can be people you know, people you have never met but know about through history, media or other means, alive or dead or mythic. Who would you invite to sit at your table, to whom you would ask, '...and what do you think?' Stay with it for as long as you need until you can picture each chair filled by someone you respect and admire.

These people now comprise your own personal Board of Elders. A feast of wisdom and resources you can draw upon for inspiration, to check out your thinking, to invite commentary. As you add them to your imaginary table, ask yourself: 'What is it that this person brings that will be of help to me?'

When you feel that you have whoever you feel needs to be there – and it needs to be said they will readily come – thank them and tell them that going forward you may decide to call a board meeting or a banquet at little notice and that you would be especially pleased if all turn up. Thank them and when you are ready, return to your sense of sitting in the chair and open your eyes. Capture what you need in your journal.

This imaginary group, and who we include in it, can change over time. People that we choose will be reflections of our own sometimes unclaimed abilities and skills that we see writ large, or larger, in someone else. Having a visual image works for some people because it can be a 'go-to' place for our own reflections, which can take us from information to wisdom if we set aside the time.

Sheila's Board of Elders

Sheila lived at the edge of a suburban spread outside the city she grew up in. Every day before work she took her two dogs for a walk in the local forest. At 5.30 in the summer mornings the sun slipped in, creating a light shimmer, even on cooler days. It always felt magical to her. Here, in the woods, she felt more aligned with her body and soul and it seemed to kick-start her day. The drive to work later was like crossing the boundary of one aspect of her life to another, and she loved it.

Another border in Sheila's life was less perceptible. It related to whether or not to put herself forward for a new leadership role at work. She was the most experienced member of her team and she was well liked throughout her workplace, a middle-sized logistics company located on the other side of the city. The other side of this border was uncharted territory for Sheila and she was not sure she had the skills, the will or the ambition to 'go for it'. When she spoke about the new role she said she knew that in order to 'go for it' she had to face her own 'dragons' before she could move forward.

Besides working on a foundation of good soil, namely, her sense of self-esteem and confidence, Sheila created a 'Board of Elders' to help remind herself of her previous experiences and talents, and to draw upon a wider palette of knowledge to help her be brave and put herself forward for the job. She knew that in order to be a good leader, which formed a central piece in her desired life garden, the borders were where she restored and resourced herself, just like her early morning walks in the forest. She also resolved to add into her design life borders such as regular meetings with friends and a local group, and that looking after those aspects of her garden framed and supported her being strong in her leadership role.

Roots of core values

This next exercise is about clarifying your core values. This is an opportunity to look at what you are doing now, or want to do, and how that aligns with the things that are of key importance to that which you are as a person, and what gives meaning to your life going forward in the design of your life garden.

Core values are a part of our root system. They drive us toward the causes, people, jobs and purposes we have as human beings. They feed what we do and who we are. When we are not in an environment that respects our values, it can create a strain on how we appear in our jobs, relationships and in the world.

Core values are part and parcel of the soil of who you are in the garden of life. We all have values but we are mostly unaware of them, except perhaps when they are challenged or we find ourselves in a situation where what is valuable to us is not aligned with the other person or the situation.

Here are some beginnings of statements. Take some time to consider what you would say to complete them:

- I feel independent when….

- I couldn't live life without….

- I feel most motivated when…

- I would stand up and speak out for…

Some values are universal values, such as principles like justice, freedom and love. Others are personal to us as individuals and can vary greatly in meaning, such as wanting to make a difference or have fun.

Try any of these if you would like to find out more about your own values:

1. Think of your ideal weekend. What would it be like? Who would you spend it with? What would you do?

2. Look back at the collection of 'lows' on the previous 'tracking your roots' exercise. What was happening back then? What made it matter so much? What was missing? What values of yours might have been affronted or dishonoured?

3. Think about your 'board of elders'. What qualities do you see lived out in those people that are resonant with who you are?

There is an exercise in Chapter 11 called 'clarifying your core values' that can help you further with this exploration.

Fred's life garden

Fred was struggling to move on in his relationships with others since his wife had left him. He felt he had done everything to keep his family going during the difficulties they faced, and he hoped it would get better, even as he found himself facing the end of his 30-year relationship. His children, teenagers, were coping as best they could. Five years on, Fred found he still could not let go of his feelings of anger. Every new relationship foundered. The soil of his relationship building had become impoverished and nothing could thrive...

Fred needed to go back to the soil and roots of who he was and enrich that before he could successfully plant new things in life. We looked back in his root system to discover how previous generations coped with difficulties they faced. He found that time and time again he came from a family that was not short of hardships but they got up, regrouped and fought again – and succeeded. This reinforced his experience that he had that bond of facing diversity in common with his ancestors and that somehow made him feel he wasn't facing this alone.

Next, Fred identified ways he could do things for himself that increased his sense of self-esteem and feelings of self worth, without focusing on looking for someone new in his life. A keen baker, he got involved in local bake-off competitions and won a few prizes. This gave him a chance to feel he was putting something back into his soul self and how he defined who he was. He met and made friends over recipe swapping. He even rediscovered a love of gardening, which had previously been his ex-wife's domain. After a while he was invited to host a column in his local paper with some of his incredible original variations on Victorian cakes. One of his children asked him to become a governor at the local primary school. He began to see himself in a different light. Others did too.

The power of intentionality in the garden's lexicon

In Tibet, people write their prayers on flags made of triangular cloth. The flags are then attached to a rope or a string and placed outside homes and temples. Every time the wind blows, the prayers flutter up into the world.

Prayer wheels are also used. A prayer is written on a scroll of paper and put inside the wheels. Then with each turn of the wheel, intentions are dispersed into the air.

A gardener has a range of intentions when designing and setting up the garden. It will show up in the overall shape, the variety and quantity of plants according to the soil variability, sun, dryness, and so on. It may be just to experiment.

We can do the same every day, every week or at different periods for different reasons with our intentionality.

When we walk in our garden with intentionality, we create sanctuary. When we go out regularly into a public green space we know and love, we help increase our levels of what Richard Louv describes as 'Vitamin N', in his book, *The Nature Principle*.[20]

Where inner meets outer

The space between the outside world and the internal world of our thoughts, feelings and sensations is like a threshold. It is a sensory threshold, barely perceptible, where you have left the tried and tested but not yet replaced it with the time between yesterday or even the last hour or minute and the next moment. We can be in the sliver of space between being comfortable and facing the edge of our own unquiet of challenge and possibility. It can be a scary place of not knowing and in that space, if we can bear to hang on a tiny bit longer, is also a place of peace and potential. Sometimes we can learn to wait out this not knowing and, with time and reflection, a new awareness can come. Sometimes, conversely, it is a call to action.

On a daily basis, like a good gardener, we can take a moment at the beginning of each day to ask ourselves: 'What's my intention for today? What do I want to bring into my day, today, in my routine, encounters with others, as I engage in my tasks and daily endeavours?' For me, this can change radically. I have an overall intention for the year and then I have a daily intention of connecting to my meditation practice. Today it was 'fun'. I decided today, in whatever I was doing, I was going to try and have fun in some way while doing it, even getting the car washed. Will this change your life? No, but in the overall design of what you want to create in your life garden it helps to give you focus, choice and control. Action follows our intention. What we pay attention to makes a difference.

When you have a sense of what your intentionality is – or perhaps you have more than one – you might like to write it on a piece of paper or capture it in some way. It can just be a single word that is significant for you, like 'light', 'ease', or 'joy'. One way to put it out to the winds of the world is to get a plant label, or stake, and a permanent marker. Write what you need to on it and stick it in your own garden as a reminder. Even in window boxes, a plant tag displaying the word of your choice that cannot be washed away by the rain is a reminder of your stake in the world too.

Permaculture

Permaculture involves conscious design in order to conserve and regenerate the earth's resources. Valuing yourself as a resource is important when considering your own life garden design.

Burnout is a state of exhaustion; physical, emotional and mental. It can include a range of symptoms, like feeling exhausted even after a good night's sleep, helplessness, hopelessness and an unending negative self-view. Everyday life becomes almost impossible in the face of chronically stressful situations.

We spoke earlier about tending the life garden. This is about befriending the garden and gardener. What goes into the ground in terms of nutrients, water, and air determines the potential health of what is planted. This is just as true for us human beings. Our conscious daring to conserve, preserve and flourish as humans depends on a number of factors.

According to Martin Seligman[21] there are five areas that help us to be in a state of flourishing. In his book *Flourish,* Seligman writes about research carried out by Felicia Huppert and Timothy So of the University of Cambridge. They defined and measured flourishing in a survey of 43,000 adults, from a representative sample of 23 European Union countries. To flourish (in terms of their definition), an individual must have all three of the core elements, which are 1) positive emotions; 2) engagement or interest (love of learning new things); and 3) meaning or purpose, generally feeling that our contribution is valuable and worthwhile. Then, of the additional features we need three of the following six, which are self-esteem, optimism, resilience, vitality, self-determination and positive relationships. They used this stringent criteria for measuring flourishing. Everything else is in service of these factors. For Seligman, these come close to the pillars of well-being theory.

It is a combination of feeling good, as well as actually having meaning, good relationships and accomplishment. The way we choose our course in life is to make the most of all six of these elements.

Do an audit of where you feel stress most acutely. Closely monitor when your personal energy tank is running too low and make sure you do what you need in order to refill it. The effects of stress over time mean we may miss or overlook some signs as they mount up.

See where you feel the least resourced and where you can make even the smallest changes every day. That may mean a better night's sleep, a proper meal if you are snacking or skipping real food, or seeing people if you're in a hermit phase.

The soil in a garden requires replenishment. Regular crops need tending, feeding, enriching, aerating, turning and digging. As humans we need nurture, fresh energy, good air, and space. There is no escape from the fact that every one of us needs this in order to thrive. It is also true that each of us is unique in the amount, variety and the way we create our personal permaculture.

Crop rotation and fallow periods

Fallow periods allow for the soil's renewal. In the garden of life, take some time to go for a walk just for the sake of it, rather than for reaching a particular target. Read something for pleasure alone, take half an hour to listen to music or just to sit quietly. Choose something outside your normal routine, even if it means taking a different route home from work, to an activity that you carry out on autopilot. You will find further suggestions for replenishing and renewing yourself by stocking up your well-being cupboard in Chapter 11.

CHAPTER 10

seeds and planting: projects and goals

Seeds and seed trays

Making changes to your life garden will require that you gather together the right tools for the job.

Seed trays are where seeds are first planted in good soil to give them the best chance of sprouting. Each one has its own compartment and gardeners put them under cover or in the best possible place, sometimes an incubator, to help them along.

Think of ideas as seeds to be planted in some prepared potting soil. Some seeds will come up and others will not. Gardeners rarely plant a single seed. They know that some will take and others may not. If many come up all at once then, in the next stage, gardeners gently pick them out and move them into more spacious pots to give them room to begin the process of establishing themselves in their own right. Your ideas are being incubated in their protective cocoon, safe until they may be ready to move on in your mind, or in your actions, should you wish to do so, ready to root and be taken to the next stage.

In your life garden, you could start by creating a file with the name of each potential new project on it. You could use a small jar or pot into which you collect things that relate to that idea. If you prefer to do this digitally, using a tool such as Pinterest, or another site or programme of your choice, that is fine. Sketch out a rough outline of the idea or scribble a few lines to begin with. Don't worry at this stage about details, or pros and cons, just a sketch of the idea for a plan, project, or activity that you might want to grow at this stage. Do one for each potential idea and create a separate file, box, jar, pot or home for it. Another way would be to treat yourself to a journal expressly for this process, a kind of 'hothouse book' for new ideas. Even a few bullet points are fine. Check your seeds regularly but not too often. Just like seeds in a tray, if you check every day you may be disappointed, because the chemistry, or alchemy, takes place over a longer time span, which requires patience and time.

Meanwhile, go about collecting more information, reading, gathering what you need in order to turn your ideas into reality. After a month, check to see which of your 'seeds' are still holding your attention, and which less so. Which ideas need more time to incubate? Which needs something else from you? When is the right moment to expose them to other perspectives and input? Be open to thought and constructive help from those who care. Be mindful to not let your ideas be talked down by well-meaning folks with their own agendas getting in the way. A concerned loved one might worry that if you take up a particular sport, for example, you will have less time together. Even with good intentions, their 'helpfulness' might feel negative when they point out the problems that could arise, rather than being fully enthusiastic for you as you might have hoped. It is not necessarily that they are against your idea but they are also for their own needs being met. People don't always speak openly about their needs. Input isn't a bad thing but if you are especially susceptible to criticism be aware that people's comments often say as much about themselves as they do about the idea itself. Be open to and robust about helpful pointers but don't let them drown you. Someone telling them it will never work, or that they don't have the skills, have been the most impactful statements on young people, who remember all their lives that someone told them at eight years of age they were no good at art, or maths, or sports, even when, years later, those words and that story are no longer valid.

Some ideas will not be viable and we may let them go for any number of reasons: motivation, finance, time or complexity. Some ideas are good but the timing is not right. For timing we can incubate an idea, just like a plant, until such time as might be appropriate.

When planting new things in your life – some tips

- Plant small – projects then have time to establish themselves further

- Consider the ultimate size and expansion of your project or life change – do you have enough space and time for something new?

- Ideally plant in Spring when the energy and verve for new ideas is high

- Prune wisely so that you are reviewing and considering the shape and size of a project as it evolves

- Consider the overall shape of the garden and its demands on you over a 12-month period

"Our job in this lifetime is not to shape ourselves into some idea we imagine we ought to be, but to find out who we are and become it"

Stephen Pressfield, *The War of Art*

Conversations with your inner gardener

All plants need three things: nitrogen to produce leaves, potassium for all flowering and fruiting plants, and phosphorus to help roots grow.

All people grow better if they are really listened to, are seen and accepted for who they are, and given the space and opportunity to set down roots of confidence in order to grow. In addition, we need courage, patience, and love. There may be other musts too for you. What are your top three elements of the highest priority that you need in order to flourish?

Different gardens need different kinds of loving care, just like people. If the garden is lucky it has a gardener who gets to know what works best and what is best reserved for special parts of the garden; for instance, to catch the sun, or to avoid it, or to have well-drained soil. If the plant doesn't survive, the gardener would rarely blame the plant. It may need a new space, a different watering and feeding regime, or to be indoors rather than outside. The best gardeners are patient, optimistic and pragmatic. Generally I find them to be among the most engaging and down-to-earth people I have ever known, and often with a magnificent sense of humour.

I am going to invite you to take a week or more to get a sense of your inner gardener. How do you look after you – this garden that is your life? Notice what works really well and what changes you might need to ask of yourself if you want to improve your gardening repertoire, time or mind set. Remember that a good outdoor gardener is discerning but compassionate.

Take your time and perhaps capture your reflections in your journal or in any way that allows you to collect your cuttings of good practice for future planting.

The flourishing gardener

Consider all the things that you enjoy doing, however small, that you find easy to do and that don't require any special effort on your part. These are different from the things you know how to do and have come to do by default, but they don't bring you any joy to do them, though they may very well have to be done, perhaps like an outdoor gardener doing the weeding. For example, you may be really good at picking colours that go well together or solving knotty problems, or helping people to feel welcome and at ease. Make a list of those and include an example that you especially remember and jot that down as well.

The wise inner gardener

This is the part of you that really knows what it knows. Sometimes you can't explain how you know something, but you do. You can call it inner wisdom, or gardener's sixth sense. It is a part of you that loves and feels compassionate towards yourself, even if sometimes you don't always want to listen. It is an inner voice that gives you the benefit of the doubt when something goes awry. It is a kind voice, very different from that of an inner critic, but there is often a truth within it that we ignore at our peril. Sometimes crops survive and thrive, sometimes we have to enrich the soil for certain plants but the earth is the earth and its properties, if well nourished with water, sun and care, will support us, hold us and allow us to grow. When our metaphorical soil is poor we can lose contact with our own deep wisdom.

Gather here what you would like to say to this part of you that is full of kindness and compassion. Where does the soil need some extra loving attention? In what ways can you listen for this truth that is yours and yours alone?

The weeding gardener

Think of this as your inner critic. What thinking patterns, unhelpful phrases and comments do you repeat to yourself that perhaps you would never say to your best friend? These thoughts get in the way of the garden growing despite its best efforts. Do keep a regular eye on this so that it doesn't get out of hand. We often have a regular litany of criticism we give ourselves, almost on automatic pilot. Like weeds, these thoughts can proliferate if we don't pay attention. Then, when we most need our courage, resilience and skills, we are choked by the weeds of negative thinking, which unchecked, know how to spread. The negative thoughts may have some truth within them, but what else could be true?

Assumptions are elixir for the weeds of the inner critic and regular attention throughout the year is essential. We all have patterns that have been there for a long time. Sometimes they trip us up so building our reservoir of weeding tools helps keep them at bay or eradicate them.

The visionary gardener

When a gardener has their hands in the earth creating a space and some depth for a new arrival, the focus is heads down. Some thinking has already happened about the necessary conditions that will help this particular plant do well. Enough sun? Too much shade? Competition with neighbouring plants? The gardener needs to think about what the plant will be like when it has reached its full size and what the other plants will be like, so a degree of vision is important to a gardener, and of course, imagination tempered with reality. A gardener aims to find balance between what he hopes the garden will look like, what he already knows about gardens, and then follows the really juicy part of getting down to the work.

Well-known celebrity gardeners such as Monty Don, Carol Klein and many others who are known to British audiences on radio, television and in magazines, display the qualities of abundant enthusiasm, steeped in acquired knowledge and experience, combining the best of childlike glee with adult professionalism.

How can you do the same for yourself in the garden of your life so that you learn from your mistakes, make use of the learning and maintain the joy of the garden as you continue to shape it?

Do some dreaming about the garden of your life. What will the next phase contain? How will you balance what cannot be changed with what can be pruned, moved, re-homed, re-positioned or simply cut out?

What good experience can you take a metaphorical cutting of so that you may replicate that experience, if not exactly, then in essence?

Dear Gardener...

This last part takes the form of a letter that you write to your own inner gardener. Whatever its ups and downs, this is *your* garden, which means that though nothing is ever certain or entirely within our control we must, at the most fundamental level, love our garden and look after and nurture it. Write this letter as a love letter or one of gratitude honouring each part, even to the critic who often starts out as a protective servant that can get out of hand and become a tyrant, even though it may no longer be needed for its original purpose. A 'thank you' note acknowledges the intention, and then you can let go of it. The weeds of our thinking can take us to task over the simplest actions, so regular attention is important.

This is not a letter for anyone but you to see, so don't hold back. What encouragement and wisdom can your inner gardener share with you? The more you garden in this way the more you will garden! When you invite your wise inner gardener to walk along with you for a stroll in the fresh air, you will create inner dialogues from a more insightful place in yourself and this will help your own inner garden to flourish.

The compost bin of life

The compost bin in a garden is the gardener's friend. It is an important resource for enriching the soil to help get the best crop of flowers, fruit or vegetables. Scraps from peeling vegetables, egg shells, the contents of the vacuum cleaner from time to time, cat hair that gets swept up, rotten fruit or vegetables, tea bags and coffee grinds. My husband adds a certain amount of grass cuttings and other garden litter. It sits and rots down. He turns it over periodically. If the local stables are offering bags of free horse manure, he is down there the minute they open, in his car, not mine, to bring back sacks of it. Like a boy in a sweet shop who has been told to help himself, he is over the moon. It all gets put into the compost bin to heat up and encourage the process of composting.

So in this mix there is only the leftover, the unwanted, the gone bad or, in the case of the horses, the eliminated vegetarian output of a day's grazing.

Far too many times I have heard clients talk more about what they can't do, are not good at, or find fault with. Or they have started something and then it fell by the wayside and the entire effort was labelled negatively.

In the compost bin of life we can make a lot better use of some of the aspects of ourselves that we discard. They may be compliments we have received from others, our skills, talents and experiences. Because we may fail, in the moment we can discount the things we do, think or get feedback that is difficult to receive.

Most of us have experiences that we would rather not remember. There may have been times we said or did the wrong thing, or failed to do anything at all when action was needed. It can be all too easy to put aside all of our bad experiences and turn away from them.

There are also terrible things that happen to individuals and families that change people for ever. We read and hear about people who have shown amazing courage in the face of terrible turns of fate, often not of their making, who somehow find the courage to get back up and find a way to create meaning, focus and intention in their lives, and sometimes, an impetus for an even bigger life than they could ever have imagined.

The story of Dorothy Johnson-Speight is an example. Dorothy's 24-year old son was murdered by a random act of gun violence in Philadelphia in the United States. While struggling with that tragedy she heard that yet another of her son's friends had been killed.

Johnson-Speight envisioned a boxing ring filled with women holding bullhorns. 'Sons,' they pleaded, 'put down your guns.'

Less than a month later, the chant became a rallying cry for other shell-shocked women in the Philadelphia area who had lost children to gun violence and wanted to join Johnson-Speight's newly formed group, Mothers in Charge. Since its formation in 2003, it has spawned sister organisations throughout the United States. Now a licensed family therapist, 'my love of my son is what drives me', says Dorothy.'This is a way I can continue to be connected to him. It's what gets me up on those rough days.'

Allan Buchmann lost his 19-year old daughter, Chitra. To honour his daughter's memory and to give other women the opportunities that Chitra lacked, Allan founded the Culture Project in 1996. His mission was to support women artists who use theatre to explore social issues, including women's issues and human rights.

Allan's goal, which was to become the foremost presenter of new work by women, took a huge leap forward when the Culture Project theatre in New York City was renamed the 'Lynn Redgrave Theater' in 2013, after the late actress.

And there is Bethany Hamilton, who was raised in a surfing family and was born to be in the water. A natural surfer, she began competing professionally as a young child. However, at 13, she lost her arm and nearly lost her life in a vicious shark attack. One month later she was back on her surfboard with a determined spirit and positive attitude. Two years later she won first place in the Explorer Women's Division of the NSSA National Surfing Championships.[22]

There are some things though, that are best put to rest. Martin, a colleague of mine, says we can either change a situation, we can change our attitude towards it, or we can remove ourselves from the path of the difficulty.[23] We have at least 51 per cent power to make some change. The importance is in choosing where we put our attention and energy. In other cases, mistakes, problems, obstacles, hardships and difficulties and the discounting of our own abilities, moments of embarrassment or shame might be the very things that contain a grain of grit that can eventually become a pearl of personal awareness or wisdom, further down the line.

So I invite you to make a list, or even create a small box, and in it, on small pieces of paper, list the things that, on reflection, you could put in your own compost bin.

Why do this? It gives you the potential to use and recycle experiences for new insights, fresh learning, and a chance to take ownership of the gems that just need extra help to grow strong and flourish.

What has been overlooked?

What may have been to put to one side?

Where have you received compliments and positive feedback and not taken them on board?

Where do you play small?

Where do you have stories about yourself that no longer serve you and could be remade into something helpful and valuable by thinking about them differently, thinking about *you* differently?

Gratitude, appreciations, a balcony view of the whole picture, some compassion for the effort you made... In this way you fertilise your garden of life so your projects can grow.

Appreciate what difficulties you have surmounted and what you have stretched yourself to do, even when...

Feel gratitude for having survived beyond the difficulty.

Have a greater awareness of what works and what doesn't.

These things can fertilise an arid garden when we bring a different mindset to them.

PART 3
harvest

CHAPTER 11

additional resources
and activities

Walking the sacred landscape cycle

Using the Five Seasons to reflect on a question

The sacred landscape cycle is a tool to help you reflect on where you are and what would help you flourish. This exercise is a five-part reflective practice model that can be adapted to use if you feel stuck with a particular issue and are curious to explore options and perspectives in order to gain greater clarity.

It can be practised with a coach or a friend, where one person asks the questions while the other person walks the sacred cycle.

A set of cards is available to accompany this process but the options offered below will also bring the exercise alive (see references at the end of this chapter).

The exercise can be done indoors or outside but ideally involves walking to a different location as you move through the seasonal positions.

This five-part cycle can happen in the course of a day, over a week or longer. When we get stuck sometimes it is because we have not taken sufficient heed of what is represented by each season of the cycle so that we achieve optimal functioning.

First take a moment to stand or sit with your feet firmly on the ground. Allow your mind and body to settle, then ask yourself what question you want to reflect on or situation you want to explore. The questions that follow are directed towards discovering more insight into the key question you are holding. That may change and evolve as you continue.

Start at the season you feel most drawn to and continue from there. Follow your intuition as to where to go next. Notice your own patterns, e.g. if you are more attracted or more tempted to linger in one season than another, or the questions in one season resonate more for you than in another. Be curious about your own process as another layer of learning.

Spring in the cycle is about energy moving outwards and upwards after the stillness of Winter. This is a time of new possibilities and beginnings. Relationships are being forged. A vision is forming. It is a time to create and be bold.

- What seeds of potential are available to you?
- What new partnerships might help?
- What needs your courage?
- What is the balance point of staying fresh and creative and being patient?

Summer energy is about maturity, ripeness, bigness and joy. It is a time of getting together with others, celebrating and full-on energy. It is the fire of excitement and of experiencing success.

- Where is the joy for you right now?

- If you were playful what would that bring into your life?

- Who or what needs to be included in the success or outcome?

Late Summer energy is about abundance and harvesting. It is about appreciating others and ourselves. It is a time to take stock and to reconnect with our core values, and nurturing ourselves.

- What can you harvest from your endeavours so far?

- What do you need to savour that you might have gone too swiftly past?

- What goodness can be preserved for the future?

- Who and what needs appreciating and nurturing?

Autumn is a time for gratitude. It is a time to extract the learning from our experiences and in some cases to say goodbye to what is now finished and acknowledge that loss with compassion. It is a time to consider what needs trimming, de-cluttering, letting go of, and re-clarifying with precision what must stay. Because life goes on this too will be part of next Spring's potential growth.

- What needs pruning or letting go of?

- What are you grateful for?

- What is really the most important thing at stake?

Winter is the time to change pace and slow down for deeper reflection to go to the heart of what is most important. It may be about connecting to something bigger than our everyday selves in terms of spirituality or soulfulness. Whatever is in Winter may be largely invisible to the eye as it is where new seeds germinate. We need a little silence for long enough to get under the surface, and to ask tougher questions of ourselves and maybe others.

- Where do you draw inspiration from?
- What's the question beneath the question that really needs addressing?
- What needs you to slow down and 'be with' rather than 'do with'?
- What does your wisest self already know?

Replenishing your Autumn well-being cupboard

Think of your Autumn cupboard as a resource you can draw on over Winter when you need some nurture and nourishment. This might be a quality you need, like extra courage or patience when you can't see your way through something but you want to explore it more. It might be something like a story you heard on the radio that makes you laugh, a poem that has always inspired you, or a small object that stands for the times when you felt really supported and held. The cupboard can contain all manner of things and is yours alone. When we are well-stocked ourselves, then our relational juice is better and stronger for others too, so for now, focus on stocking or re-stocking your own cupboard.

In gardening terms, this is your well-equipped Winter shed. Your job is to fill it with what you need and what you know works for you, when you need some extra support and resources. Like a shed, it will contain a range of different tools and processes, depending on what is required. Of course, although this is your Winter store, you can access it at any time throughout the year. The prerequisite is that when you open the cupboard, everything inside contributes to your overall well-being, physically, mentally or spiritually, at some time or another. Awareness and intention together are a powerful combination.

Your task is to stock your cupboard before Winter begins, so ideally, if you have not been gathering things for it over the year, then it is good to start no later than the cusp between the end of Autumn and the start of Winter. Be mindful of keeping it topped up, however – you can add to your cupboard at any time.

Begin this exercise by closing your eyes and thinking about what you could put inside your Autumn cupboard. Have a pen and paper or your journal nearby to capture thoughts and ideas on what it might contain. Think about:

Qualities that are important to you, written on a piece of beautiful card

Poems, stories, cartoons, jokes, quotes

Letters or cards you have received or that have meant a lot to you

Goodies (anything that is relatively small, stroke-able, or that makes you smile)

Photographs of people, places or experiences that fill you with positive emotions

A small object that represents something important to you

A small treat of some kind

A memory of when you really tackled a tough time in your life and you made it through (write it down too)

Some lists written on the most beautiful paper you can find that answer these questions

In the last 11 months:

- What made you smile?
- What surprised you?
- What gifts did the last 11 months give you?

Thinking in threes

What three things:

- Are you most proud of?
- Will you do to be kind to yourself?
- Will you cherish in your home and garden?

Then find a way to keep these things where you can get to them easily. You might keep them in a virtual file, or you might like to create a box especially to house the more physical elements; for example, a special item that might be small in size but huge in meaning, or even a bar of your favourite special chocolate or some little treat. As in most cases, keeping this well-stocked is the point. You may not need it all and you can decide to replace some or all of it each year as Winter rolls around. It is there now for the times you just need a little something more.

Our five senses

Every day we are bombarded by the excessive sensory input of urban life, a lot of it digital. Our senses show us a way into greater present-moment awareness of how amazing we are as humans, and we can use these highly tuned parts of ourselves to gain greater understanding of ourselves and the world around us.

Sight

Taking a fresh look at what and how we see can help us appreciate what is right in front of us. Our brain is sophisticated so it organises what we see, making it easier to recognise patterns, so we can tell at a glance that the lump of soft white stuff on top of a tan cone-shaped object is an ice cream. This filtering, however normal for us all, means we might miss seeing things as we go about our daily business.

Activity

Find a place in your garden or patio. Keep your eyes open and simply notice what is in your field of vision. You might see shadows, lines, light as it reflects across surfaces, clouds in the distance... Sit for a few minutes then take a quarter turn to your right and repeat the exercise. Keep repeating the exercise a quarter turn at a time until you are back in your original position. Take a further few minutes to look from above to below you and from below to above you. What did you discover?

Finally, before you stop, take a moment or two to note what stood out for you.

Sound

Sounds constantly surround us, whether by our choosing through conversation and music, or through the world around us conducting daily business, like trains, planes, cars, birds and machines. We can be unaware though of sounds that are in our lives; for instance, the clock on the mantelpiece, or the flowing water as you wash up a cup or plate. Some people can sleep through traffic noise, voices, rain, and wind while others are startled awake by the merest sound. A mother even in deep sleep wakens to the sound of her newborn baby crying.

Sound can be emotional: a friend crying, the belly laughter of a group of people enjoying a good joke, the purr of our cat sitting next to us.

Activity

Take a sound walk. The purpose is to be completely present to all that you can hear. Start by imagining opening your ears wide and walk for a while, listening for sounds that are near, midrange, and as far away as possible. When it feels a good place to do so, stop and listen to sounds with your eyes closed.

This can be a good activity to try when you are indoors and feel stressed or caught up in unhelpful thoughts. Close your eyes and focus on what you can actually hear.

Taste

Taste is a remarkable tool for learning. Infants will put almost anything in their mouths as a way to learn about it. The tongue can identify five basic taste groups: bitter, salty, sweet, sour and savoury. There are a few more besides. Because the senses of smell and taste are so connected, sometimes just smelling something we know we like gives us a sense of almost eating it. Texture makes a difference, how foods feel in the mouth and on our lips. We can sense metallic, watery and fatty tastes too.

Activity

Gather something from each taste group on a plate: something sweet, sour, salty, savoury, and bitter. Close your eyes and taste each one very slowly and notice what happens in your mouth and in you as you do so. To make this activity a bit more challenging, do it with a friend and each of you collect an item from each group but do not reveal them to your partner in this experiment. Take turns trying out the items as they are given to you by the other person. See if you are as good at guessing what you are eating without the visual information of seeing the food.

Alternatively, pick items with very different textures and taste each piece of food very slowly, exploring the different sensations with your tongue and teeth.

Smell

Smells have a strong impact on many people. It is quite possible we remember the smell of things that we may not have been around for years. Smells can strongly evoke a time and place. Smell tells us when something is burning or might be toxic. Smell makes us smile when our noses connect with something really pleasant like a rose or the smell of food we love. Each season evokes a different smell: fresh blossom in Spring, freshly mowed grass in Summer, baling hay in Late Summer, bonfires in Autumn and freshly fallen snow in Winter. Smells can transport us to different places and times. The thalamus picks up aromas and odours and takes them to regions in the brain involved in learning and memory.[23]

Activity

1) Take a few samples of teas, coffees or food or drink, such as spices or whiskies or types of wine, that are emotive for you and put a bit in separate cups. Close your eyes and sample the smell of each.

2) Take a walk in the season you are in and see what smells are most evocative of that season for you.

Interestingly, when it comes to metaphors for smell there are more negative connotations for smell than for the other four senses. Can you think of some?

Touch

The sense of touch is right in the present moment. We can't touch something with our hands that happened last week. Skin receptors transmit information via the nervous system to the brain. Our skin is the largest organ of the body and each part has the capacity to feel something. It is the first sense as humans we develop in the womb.

Activity

As you go on a regular walk touch familiar natural objects around you – the bark of trees, the leaves of bushes and plants, the metal of a park bench, the dew resting on a leaf. Feel the grass and if it is warm enough to do so, take off your shoes and socks and feel the ground and the grass beneath your feet. Pay attention to the wind on your face or a leaf brushing your arm as you walk.

See **www.fletcherprentice.com/savour** for a more detailed exploration into the senses.

Clarifying your core values

Your personal or core values are a central part of who you are – and who you want to be. By becoming more aware of these important factors in your life, you can use them as a guide to make the best choice in any situation.

When you define and name your core values, you discover what's truly important to you. They may be values that you have always had or ones that have evolved over time and through your life experiences. A good way to clarify what your values are is to look back and identify when you felt really good, and confident that you were making good choices in your life.

As you go through the questions, reflect on examples from both your career and personal life. This will help you get some balance in your answers.

Step1: Identify when you were happiest

- What were you doing?
- Were you with other people? Who?
- What other factors contributed to your happiness?

Step 2: Identify the times when you were most proud

- Did other people share your pride? Who?
- What other factors contributed to your feelings of pride?

Step 3: Describe the times you felt most satisfied and fulfilled

- What need or desire was fulfilled?
- How and why did the experience give your life meaning?
- What other factors contributed to your feeling of fulfilment?

Step 4: Determine your top values based on your experience of happiness, meaning and fulfilment

- What makes each experience truly important and memorable? Use the following list of common personal values to help you get started. Aim for ten values. As you work through the list, you might find that some naturally combine together; for example, if you value helping society, community, and generosity, you might say that service to others is one of your top values.

Abundance
Accountability
Accuracy
Achievement
Adventurousness
Adaptability
Altruism
Ambition
Assertiveness
Authenticity

Balance
Beauty
Belonging
Boldness
Brilliance

Calmness
Carefulness
Caring
Challenge
Change
Cheerfulness
Clear-mindedness
Commitment
Community
Compassion
Competitiveness
Connection

Consciousness
Consistency
Contentment
Continuous Improvement
Contribution
Control
Conviction
Cooperation
Courage
Creativity
Credibility
Curiosity

Daring
Decisiveness
Dependability
Determination
Diligence
Discipline
Discretion
Diversity
Dynamism

Economy
Effectiveness
Efficiency
Elegance
Empathy
Enjoyment

Enthusiasm
Equality
Excellence
Excitement
Expertise
Exploration
Expressiveness

Fairness
Faith
Family-orientation
Fidelity
Fitness
Flexibility
Fluency
Focus
Freedom
Friendship
Fun

Generosity
Goodness
Grace
Gratitude
Growth

Happiness
Hard Work
Health

Helping Society
Honesty
Honour
Humility

Independence
Ingenuity
Inner Harmony
Integrity
Intellect
Introspection
Intuition

Justice

Kindness

Legacy
Love
Loyalty

Making a Difference
Mastery
Meaning

Obedience
Open-mindedness
Optimism
Order

Perfection
Popularity
Positivity
Practicality
Professionalism
Prudence

Quality-orientation

Reflection
Reliability
Religion
Resourcefulness
Results-oriented
Rigour

Security
Self-actualisation
Self-control
Selflessness
Self-reliance
Self-respect
Serenity
Service
Shrewdness
Simplicity
Speed
Spontaneity
Stability

Status
Strategic Thinking
Structure
Success
Support

Teamwork
Thoroughness
Thoughtfulness
Timeliness
Tolerance
Traditionalism
Trustworthiness

Understanding
Uniqueness
Usefulness

Vision
Vitality

Warmth
Well-being
Wisdom

5: Prioritise your top values

Now put your pen down and take a moment to reflect on what you have selected. Looking a little deeper is the next step. You will be prioritising the order of importance of your core values. This will also give you a sense of what speaks to you the most.

- First write down your top values, not in any particular order.

- Then, look at the first two values and ask yourself: 'If I could satisfy only one of these, which would I choose?' It might help to visualise a situation in which you would have to make that choice. Work through the list, by comparing each value with another, until your list is in the correct order for you.

- What would your top three be? These form the very basis of your principles and your way of seeing life.

Step 6: Reaffirm your values

- Review your choices and make sure that they fit with your life and your vision for yourself.

- Do these values make you feel good about yourself?

- Are you proud of your top three values?

- Would you be comfortable and proud to talk about or stand up for your values to people you respect and admire?

- Do these values represent things you would support, even if your choice isn't popular, and it puts you in the minority?

Consider your values and how they play out in all aspects and choices in your life, including making decisions. When we are aligned with our core values, our sense of integrity and what we know is right is clearer, and this contributes to confidence in ourselves and how congruent we are perceived by others.

Further resources

https://thehappinesstrap.com

Includes a free values questionnaire as well as other free resources.

www.authentichappiness.sas.upenn.edu/testcenter

The University of Pennsylvania offers a range of free questionnaires, including happiness and life satisfaction and a values / strengths questionnaire. The authentic happiness education centre is linked to the work of Martin Seligman and his colleagues in the field of positive psychology.

www.viacharacter.org/www/Character-Strengths-Survey

The Values in Action Institute also offers a free 15-minute values questionnaire.

Create a relationship heat map

Get two pads of Post-it notes or index cards in different colours, and a pen. Use either a large A1 flipchart size sheet of paper or a blank wall where you can stick the Post-it notes or tape the cards.

Draw a central circle on your sheet or wall space and create a compass shape. Mark the top of the paper as North. This is the 'hottest' point. In the opposite direction mark South, representing no heat at all; 'cold'. West and East stand for mid-points between the two. Draw lines between points N and S and one between W and E.

Consider the activities you engaged in alone or with others last Summer at home, work, with your community, or in whatever group setting you may be associated with. Take a moment to scan through those moments that come to mind.

Using one colour of Post-it per activity, task, or event, write on each note things that made you feel exhilarated, in flow, joyful, or really alive and wholehearted. You could assign it a number if that helps. For instance, at '10' you are so joyful you almost float off, or bounce with energy, enjoying the moment fully. Use this colour Post-it for anything marked from 6 up to 10 for all the tasks/events that fit into this category and assign them a numerical value.

Use the other colour Post-it notes for activities you score anywhere from 0 (meaning it is just a chore you had to get through) and up to 5 (meaning it is fine to do at the time but you wouldn't look for more of the same). Place them on South at the bottom of the diagram.

Now do the same for all the other activities that score between 2 and 9. Decide the degree of warmth, or joy or compassion they each generate and therefore which colour Post-it is needed. Place these in your map between North and South.

You can do this exercise purely about work or home or compare the two. You decide where the value lies for you.

When you are ready, put all the Post-it notes or cards on the chart, or the wall. Those scoring 9 down to 6 are on the East side of the map and those 5 to 0 on the West side.

If you do this as a couple it can be helpful to choose different colours so you can spot the different groupings when you review your heat map after you complete the task. You can also do this in a linear way. Draw three columns on a sheet of paper and divide your activities as 'warm', 'neutral down to negative', and 'hot'. When you are done look at the columns to see which activities need to come off, stay as they are, you wish to do more of, or do less of.

Greenhousing point:

Stand back and look at any patterns.

What is true for you?

What can you learn from doing this?

What will that mean for you either this Summer or for the next?

Befriend a tree

Think of a place in nature you know or love that you can get to easily. Over the next 12 months, on one of your walks, find a tree that particularly draws your attention. It could be a yew tree in a churchyard, an ancient oak in the woods or any kind of well established tree. Throughout the year, visit the tree and get to know it as it changes over the seasons. Notice the total shape of the tree as it moves in and out of leaf, the angle of its branches and twigs, the smell of its bark after rain, the translucency of its leaves in Spring, the soft hue changes as August gives way to September, or the crinkle in Autumn.

Use your senses. Touch the tree gently and feel the bark on the trunk, watching out for any insects that could be camouflaged there. Generally, the bigger and older the tree, the more wildlife it can be home to, even temporarily. Does your tree show any marks of history on it? Perhaps the scorch marks of lightning, or something stuck in it that is manmade, like a nail? Would you know it from all the other trees around it?

Inspired by The Wildlife Trust's member magazine *Local Wildlife*, Summer 2019 issue

"Trees are poems that the earth writes upon the sky"

Kahlil Gibran

Introduction to mindfulness practice

The first thing to say is that you don't need to sit on a cushion or spend an hour a day in meditation to be a mindfulness practitioner. It is true that regularity is important, so start small if you have never tried this before. Five minutes a day for six days a week is a good start. Build from there. If you can build up to even 15-20 minutes practice, six days a week you will begin to develop a skill that can support you throughout your life. Mindfulness is not about trying to get somewhere else, but simply being aware of where you are, and allowing yourself to be where and as you are.

There is a growing body of research that demonstrates the effectiveness of mindfulness practice on our health. You can find hundreds of articles online, and even more books available.

Here are a few exercises that can help you begin.

In Part 1 of this book you will have found a number of invitations to walk throughout the five seasons and each of the dedicated Postcards from the Hedgerow included an invitation to really look, hear, and smell as you walk, connecting to what is in the present moment, putting aside the busy and active mind that is constantly somewhere else in time, rather than the present moment.

By becoming more aware of our bodily sensations, feelings and thoughts from moment to moment, we give ourselves the possibility of greater freedom and choice; we do not have to play out the same old patterns that may have caused us problems in the past.

Our aim is to increase awareness so that we can respond to situations with choice, rather than react automatically. We do this by practising becoming more aware of where our attention is and deliberately bringing the focus of attention back into our body and senses, over and over again.

Mindfulness of breathing – instructions

Sit in a comfortable posture, with your spine erect and let your shoulders drop.

Close your eyes if it feels comfortable.

Bring your awareness to your body sensations, by focusing your attention on the sensations of touch and pressure in your body where it makes contact with the floor and whatever you are sitting on. Spend a few minutes exploring these sensations. Bring your attention to your belly, feeling it rise or expand gently on the in-breath and fall or recede on the out-breath.

Keep the focus on your breathing, 'being with' each in-breath for its full duration and with each out-breath for its full duration, as if you were riding on the waves of your own breathing.

Every time that you notice that your mind has wandered off the breath, softly note what it was that took you away, and then gently escort your attention back to your belly and the feeling of the breath coming in and out.

If your mind wanders from the breath a thousand times, then your 'job' is simply to bring it back to the breath every time, no matter what it becomes preoccupied with. It is just as valuable to become aware that your mind has wandered and bring it back to the breath as it is to remain aware of the breath.

(Adapted from Jon Kabat-Zinn, *Full Catastrophe Living*)

Basics of sitting meditation

It helps to adopt an erect and dignified posture, with our head, neck and back aligned vertically – this is the physical manifestation of the inner attitudes of self-reliance, self-acceptance, patience and alert attention that we are cultivating.

Practise on a chair or on the floor. If you use a chair, choose one that has a straight back and that allows your feet to be flat on the floor. If at all possible, sit away from the back of the chair so that your spine is self-supporting.

If you choose to sit on the floor, do so on a firm thick cushion (or pillow folded over once or twice) which raises your buttocks off the floor three to six inches.

You can also use a meditation stool which can be made or you can buy online. Ideally, when you are sitting on either a meditation cushion or stool, your knees should be lower than your hips. The most important factor is that whichever you choose – chair, floor, cushion or stool – you are stable, comfortable and can maintain your sitting position as the length of time you sit increases.

You can use the next exercise to begin practising with. Read it into your mobile telephone so you can replay it when you want to use it.

There are a number of good on-the-go mobile apps for this purpose, including:

www.headspace.com/headspace-meditation-app

www.headspace.com

www.calm.com

https://insighttimer.com

The latter is one of the most widely used free apps, which includes over a thousand recorded meditation exercises lasting from one minute to one hour to try out, and a timer function if you just want to do your own thing.

"To allow ourselves to be truly in touch with where we already are, no matter where that is, we have got to pause in our experience long enough to let the present moment sink in; long enough to actually feel the present moment, to see it in its fullness, to hold it in awareness and thereby come to know and understand it better."

Jon Kabat-Zinn, *Wherever You Go, There You Are*

Purposefully create daily moments of presence

Engaging in everyday activities with intentional attention is an act of mindfulness. When we bring intentional attention to what we are doing in any moment, we are bringing our full attention, thoughts, feelings and body in full alignment with what we are experiencing, with the awareness that we are doing so. This could be washing the dishes, brushing our teeth, walking to the train station, getting dressed, having a shower or making a cup of coffee. So if you are washing dishes, put your full attention on this, taking the time to really feel into that single experience; the warm water on your hands, the feel of the objects as you pick them up, maybe even the smell of the bubbles. Keep bringing your mind back to the activity when it strays to think about something else.

Other options might be taking a different route home from work, eating lunch in a different location or packing a lunch that is different from that you normally eat, so you can be even more awake and aware with your attention on your experience.

There is a growing body of research about how this intentional attention benefits our emotional well-being and even positively affects our brain's chemistry. The Frontiers of Human Neuroscience article 'Effects of mindful attention and compassion meditation training on amygdala response to emotional stimuli in an ordinary non-meditative state....' outlines a number of their findings.
www.ncbi.nlm.nih.gov/pmc/articles/PMC3485650/

Useful website addresses

While meditation on your own is absolutely possible, the support of a community can be a great help. There are many centres throughout the country that teach secular or spiritual mindfulness practices.

For secular centres that teach eight-week Mindfulness Based Stress Reduction (MBSR) or Mindfulness Based Cognitive Therapy (MBCT), check your local directories.

www.bangor.ac.uk/mindfulness

The Centre for Reflective Practice at Bangor can help you find eight-week MBSR programmes.

www.oxfordmindfulness.org

and the Oxford Centre for Mindfulness can help you find an eight-week MBCT course and offers other trainings and workshops in mindfulness practices.

www.themindfuness-solution.com

Offers information, downloadable mindfulness practices and further resources.

www.wisebrain.org

The Well Spring Institute, a not-for-profit organisation, was created to help people learn new ways to change the brain for the better, for more happiness, love and wisdom. The website has many articles, free resources and tools for mindfulness.

www.gaiahouse.co.uk

A meditation centre and silent retreat house in the woodlands of Devon.

Further reading

Brach T. (2013). *True Refuge*. London, Hay House.

Chodrön P. (2016). *When Things Fall Apart: Heart Advice for Difficult Times.* Boulder, Shambhala.

Hahn TN. (1975). *The Miracle of Mindfulness*. London, Rider Press.

Hanson R. (2009). *Buddha's Brain*. California, New Harbinger Publications.

Kabat-Zinn J. (2013). *Full Catastrophe Living*. London, Piatkus Press.

Kabat-Zinn J. (2004). *Wherever You Go There You Are.* London, Little Brown Group.

Kornfield J. (2002 revised ed). *A Path with Heart*. New York, Rider Press.

Salzburg S. (2002). *Real Love: The Art of Mindful Connection*. US, Shambhala Publications.

Santorelli S. (1999). *Heal Thyself*. New York, Three Rivers Press.

Siegel R. (2010). *The Mindfulness Solution: Everyday Practices For Everyday Problems*. New York, Guilford Press.

Silverstone S. (2012). *The Mindfulness Breakthrough.* London, Watkins Publishing.

Williams M., Penman D. (2012). *Mindfulness, a Practical Guide to Finding Peace in a Frantic World*. London, Piaktus.

"Fill the paper with breathings of your heart"

William Wordsworth

Journal writing

Here are some ideas to help you begin capturing your thoughts in a journal. Writing even a small amount several times a week keeps you in tune with the journal writing mindset. You'll find you are noticing your internal world more, expressing it and staying in touch with yourself.

Preparation

Choose a notebook or blank journal and a selection of pens that feel good to write with. You might prefer to have a few colours to ring the changes and moods in your writing. There are advantages to writing by hand. The pace of writing, or drawing, by hand slows you down and gives you more time for thoughts to come in. A nice variation is to deliberately write, or draw, as slowly as you can – it's so different from the usual way we get information out, through texts or emails or other social media. If you decide you really want to write on a tablet, then create a file that will be solely for your journaling. But try and experiment with writing by hand, if you can.

One way to get into the mood for journal writing is to quiet your mind, centre yourself, and allow yourself to relax. There are many ways to get to that quiet place. You may have a particular place in your home where the bustle of the day can be put aside briefly. It might be that you like writing amid the anonymous bustle of a café, or you prefer to listen to some calming music or to the sounds of nature.

You might try listening to different pieces of music before you journal and see if and how it affects your writing. You can create your own **journaling playlist** with some of your own favourites. Some people like to read a poem to themselves before they begin and still others just like the spontaneity of picking up their journal, anywhere, anytime and just writing for a set, short piece of time wherever they are. *When you don't have much time to write, that is the perfect time for the five-minute journal entry.* The choice is as individual as you are.

Find a place to sit down and relax. Take five slow in-breaths and five even longer out-breaths so you really settle before you start.

Beginning

You may find that getting started is easy or you may need some extra momentum when the blank page stops you in your tracks, or you are not sure what to write about... Here are some ways that might be helpful. Even regular writers use these when they need to move from a place of 'I don't know what to write' to a flow on paper or screen.

1. Writing prompts

Prompts are words, images or topics that are designed to just get us going. Writing prompts can be absolutely diverse and not necessarily have anything to do with the actual topic you have in mind. Examples include the following:

Describe the first image that pops into your mind as your pen touches the paper or as your fingers touch the keyboard. Describe that image, even if it is blankness or confusion or 'nothing'. Describe it in detail, writing about what other things it reminds you of, and follow that thread until you are ready to stop. No need to be serious, funny, ponderous, perceptive, witty, if you don't want to be. There are 'no have to's' here. That's one of the beauties of keeping a journal. Whatever you write is right!

Open a book and pick a random word and use that as a prompt to start writing. Write about what that word evokes for you, whatever it is. Remember this is just to get the writing juices flowing.

Pick an image in a magazine or from a collection of pictures that you have and like. You can collect some and keep them in a file for when you need a writing prompt.

Pick a question that draws you. In each of the chapters of this book you find many questions. Choose one that draws you and just begin.

How am I right now? Start with the present moment – what's going on right now? Start with a feeling or start with a story: 'Today the funniest thing happened...'

Draw an image: add something that isn't just words into your journal entry. Doodle. Draw how you feel. Or draw an animal (whether real or imaginary) that describes a situation that you find yourself in. No one but you will see it. Laugh. Play.

Journal writing can be lighthearted and fun. You can use your journal to inject some joy into an otherwise frustrating or tiring day. Draw a quick picture of your irritations or capture an image of a place that makes you feel calm and peaceful.

Add colours and/or abstract images, doodles even, that appear by letting your hand do the 'thinking'and just see what evolves when you give yourself a little time to draw. Keep it light, fun, and non-critical.

And if you want to go beyond doodling, art journaling is a craft in itself. There are entire publications devoted to teaching about art journaling that are filled with creative ideas. See the further resources list below.

Make a list. For example, what you ate during the last two hours, or a list of five things you saw, heard, smelled, tasted or touched, or about an article or programme that you watched, read or listened to.

Collecting items. Anything you come across in daily life is great for a journal – it could be the ticket stub for a play you saw, a leaf that you were attracted to on a walk, a feather or anything that you want to keep for its interest, shape, and colour or just because...

2. Free writing

Free writing has three rules:

Rule one is that you write for a specific period of time, like five, seven or ten minutes.

Second, once the time begins you don't stop writing, or lift your pen from the paper until the time is up, even if you are writing 'I-don't-what-to-write, blah, blah blah...' The point is to keep your pen moving and get your hand, heart, eye and pen engaged as one. You can outsmart the dreaded 'journal block' by writing so fast that your inner critic can't keep up.

The third rule is that you do not stop to edit, correct, or re-read what you have written. That allows your inner critic to start taking over. The purpose of free writing is to get you into flow. Later on, if you wish, you can re-read your writing but if we do that in the middle of a piece of free writing we inhibit our own expression at that moment.

Don't have time for even five minutes? Just write SIX WORDS that describe your day. Six pithy, meaningful words that describe your day....That's it! (It can be a list of six words, or a concise sentence.

Here is an example of a six-word journal entry: *Inspiration. Snowflakes. Fireplace. Breathe. Listen. Dream.*

"My aim is to put down on paper what I see and what I feel in the best and simplest way"

Ernest Hemingway

Protect your privacy

Store your journal in its own special place so that the temptation for others to read is diminished. Ask for agreement with your housemates that your journal is private. Reserve the first page of any new journal for your name and phone number or e-mail address, along with a notice: This is my personal journal. Please do not read it without my permission. If none of that would stop whoever might read your journal, get a shredder. Find a creative way to protect your privacy, such as a new email account with a fresh password, from which to write to yourself. Or keep your journal on a flash drive. Make your privacy an intentional act.

Finally, if there is one absolute rule of journal writing, it is that there simply are no real rules. Do what works for you. Don't worry about what you're not doing. Give yourself permission to enjoy the process.

"The act of writing is the act of discovering what you believe"

David Hare

Health and journal writing

In their 2016 book, *Opening Up by Writing it Down: How Expressive Writing Improves Health and Eases Emotional Pain*, James Pennebaker and Joshua M. Smith summarised expressive writing studies they had been conducting since 1986, where groups of students at the University of Texas were split into two groups. One group were assigned to write about their deepest thoughts, emotions and traumas, and the other to write on superficial topics. Blood was drawn from the participants before and after the study, which led researchers to find that those who wrote about their traumas and emotions had 'enhanced immune function' compared with those who wrote about superficial topics.

In the UK, similar studies with people who had recently experienced a heart attack or myocardial infarction were asked to write about their thoughts and feelings related to their heart attacks. These showed a decrease in prescribed medications, fewer reported cardiac symptoms and lower diastolic pressure five months after disclosure intervention was over.

James W. Pennebaker is the Regents Centennial Professor of Liberal Arts and Executive Director

https://liberalarts.utexas.edu/psychology/faculty/pennebak

Building on this research, researchers John Allen and Matthias Mehl at the University of Arizona, in a study of 109 men and women, found that keeping a journal after a divorce not only helped people make sense of the experience emotionally and move forward, but also resulted in lower heart rate and higher heart rate variability, associated with better health.

https://uanews.arizona.edu/story/narrative-journaling-may-help-hearts-health-postdivorce

Further online resources

www.journal therapy.com

This is the centre for life-based writing for healing, growth and change. This is a good resource if you want to take journal writing further and deeper.

www.iajw.com

The International Association of Journal Writing courses, articles, support, and events.

www.jackee holder.com

Author, coach and leader in her field, Jackee Holder offers a range of free resources as well as access to her blogs and events, all designed to expand and support a lifelong passion for journaling herself and for helping others discover their voice and themselves through journaling. She regularly runs a four-week Paper Therapy journaling class, and introduces a range of creative journaling prompts delivered twice a week online.

Books

Cohn K. (ed) (2017). *Art Journal Kick Starter*. F&W Media (Creative Mixed Media).

Czikszentmihalyi M. (2002). *Flow: The Psychology of Happiness. The classic work on how to achieve happiness.* Rider Press, London.

Geiss C., Jessup C. (2002). *The Inner and Outer Method*. California, New World Library.

Miller B., Hughes H. (2012). *The Pen and the Bell: Mindful Writing in a Busy World*. MA, Skinner House Books.

Mindfulness Project (2016). *I Am Here Now: a Creative Mindfulness Guide and Journal*. New York, Tarcher Perigree Press.

Neuberger E. (2018). *Journal Sparks.* Storey Publishing, STK Edition.

Patel M L. (2015). *Start Where You Are*. New York, Tarcher Perigree Press.

Pennebaker JP, Evans J. (2014). *Expressive Writing, Words that Heal*. Idyll Arbor.

Pennebaker JP, Smith JM. (2016). *Opening Up by Writing it Down: How Expressive Writing Improves Health and Eases Emotional Pain*. New York, Guildford Press.

Smith K. (2013). *Wreck This Journal*. London, Penguin.

Keep this finger labyrinth on your desk. When you are stressed and need to relax, use your finger to slowly trace a path into the centre and then back out to the entrance. The spiralling path of the labyrinth teaches us to slow down and refocus, and leads us to feeling more centred and balanced.

REFERENCES

Part 1

1. Durrell L. (1988). *Spirit of Place: Mediterranean Writings* edited by A.G. Thomas. London, Faber & Faber p.53.

2. Jung C. (1969). *The Collected Works of C.G. Jung Vol. 11.* London, Routledge & Kegan Paul.

3. For further reading, see Wu Hsing Henderson J. Wuxing (Wu-hsing): Five Phases in Antonio S. Cua (ed.) (2003). *Encyclopedia of Chinese Philosophy*. New York, Routledge, pp.786-88 and Maciocia G. (2005). *The Foundations of Chinese Medicine* (2nd ed.). London, Elsevier Ltd.

4. O'Donohue J. (1997). *Anam Cara: Spiritual Wisdom from the Celtic World*. London, Bantam Books p.118.

5. Goleman D. (1996). *Emotional Intelligence: Why It Can Matter More Than IQ*. London, Bantam Books. For more information, also see *What Happens in the Brain When We Feel Fear* by Arash V. Javanbakht and Linda Saab, both Assistant Professors of Psychiatry, Wayne University. 26 October 2017 *'The Conversation'* [Online] www.Smithsonian.com and *Calming your brain during conflict* by Diane Musho Hamilton. 22 Dec 2015 Harvard Business Review [Online] https://hbr.org/2015/12/calming-your-brain-during-conflict

6. Yin Yang is the concept of duality forming a whole. There are two forces in the universe, according to Chinese theory: Yin is the passive, negative force, and Yang the active, positive force. We encounter examples of Yin and Yang every day. As examples: night (Yin) and day (Yang), female (Yin) and male (Yang). The symbol for Yin Yang is called the Taijitu. Most people just call it the yin yang symbol in the west. The Taijitu symbol has been found in more than one culture and over the years has come to represent Taoism. For more information see also: Lawrence R. (2002). *Little Book of Yin and Yang*. Dorset, Element Books; Wang R and Yinyang R. (2012). *The Way of Heaven and Earth in Chinese Thought and Culture (New Approaches to Asian History)*. Cambridge, Cambridge University Press; and John A. (2013). *Dancing With the Yin and Yang*. Colorado, Polaris Press.

7. See https://www.toolshero.com/toolsheroes/abraham-maslow Maslow, A. H. (2013). *A Theory of Human Motivation*. Start Publishing LLC.

8. See https://www.goodreads.com/author/quotes/16823.Michael_Jordan

9. Lannon R., Amini F., Lewis T. (2001). *A General Theory of Love*. New York: Random House.

10. Rizzolatti G., Craighero L. (2004). *The Mirror Neuron System. Annual Review*. Department of Neuroscience, University of Parma, Italy p. 104.

A mirror neuron is a neuron which fires both when an animal performs an action and when the animal observes the same action performed by another (especially animals in the same species). These neurons have been observed in primates, including humans, and in some birds.

Mirror neurons are one of the most important discoveries in the last decade of neuroscience. These are a variety of visio-spatial neurons which indicate fundamentally about human social interaction. Essentially, mirror neurons respond to actions that we observe in others. The interesting part is that mirror neurons fire in the same way when we actually recreate that action ourselves. Apart from imitation, they are responsible for myriad other sophisticated human behaviour and thought processes.

See also: Iacoboni M, (2009). *Mirroring People, The Science of How we Connect to Others*. New York, Picador. Marco Iacoboni, a neuroscientist at the University of California at Los Angeles, is best known for his work on mirror neurons [Online] https://www.scientificamerican.com/article/the-mirror-neuron-revolut/

[11.] The concept of limbic resonance was advanced in the book *A General Theory of Love* (see ref.9 above). It is one of the concepts central to the book's premise: that our brain chemistry and nervous systems are measurably affected by those closest to us (**limbic resonance**) and that our systems synchronise with one another in a way that has profound implications for personality and lifelong emotional health (**limbic regulation**); and that these set patterns can be modified through therapeutic practice (**limbic revision**). In other words, this is our capacity for empathy and non-verbal connection. It forms and informs the basis of our social connections.

[12.] www.livescience.com (2015) Oxytocin: Facts about the Cuddle Hormone by Stephanie Pappas

[13.] Hanson R (2014). *Hardwiring Happiness*. London, Rider Books.

[14.] Siegel R.D. (2009). *The Mindfulness Solution: Everyday Practices for Everyday Problems*. London, Guilford Press. Visit www.themindfuness-solution.com where you can download a free mp3 copy of The Raisin Meditation.

[15.] Wu Wei – the fertile void. There are always tasks that you must exert effort to finish whether it is a work issue, home maintenance or looking after the kids. And there are some valuable things in life which cannot be achieved by simply trying harder; what's more, efforts to achieve them can often be self-defeating, like planning to be spontaneous or not thinking of a green elephant. Or in the case of much bigger objectives like seeking happiness and love, where trying too hard can have a negative impact.

Wu wei is a concept literally meaning non-action, non-doing or non-forcing. It is not about doing nothing. It is action that does not involve struggle or excessive effort. Wu wei is the cultivation of a mental state in which our actions are quite effortlessly in alignment with the flow of life.

For more information see:

www.the-taoism-for-modern-world.com/simple-steps-wu-wei-not-doing/

www.snsociety.org/effortless-practice-wu-wei/

Part 2

[16.] Balles T. (2004). *Dancing the Ten Thousand Things*. Nebraska, iuniverse p.96.

[17.] What if! Ltd. (2002). *Sticky Wisdom*. London, Capstone Publishing pp.47-77.

[18.] Buzan T., Buzan B. (1993). *The Mind Map Book*. London, BBC Books.

[19.] O'Connor F. (eds. Fitzgerald S & R) (1970). *Mystery and Manners: Occasional Prose*. New York, Farrar Straus & Giroux.

[20.] Louv R. (2012). *The Nature Principle*. New York, Algonquin Books p.82. Louv writes a whole chapter on Vitamin N. One of his references is Janet Ady of the US Fish and Wildlife Service speaking at a conference of grassroots leaders trying to connect people to the importance of restorative nature spaces for wellbeing: in other words get outdoors and increase vitamin N – nature.

21. Seligman, MEP. (2011). *Flourish: A New Understanding of Happiness and Well-Being and How to Achieve Them*. London, Nicholas Brealey.

22. For more on Bethany Hamilton and other inspiring stories, see: www.beliefnet.com/entertainment/sports/galleries/5-inspiring-athletes-who-overcame-disabilities

23. In conversation with Martin Longdon, The Coaching Hothouse.

24. See www.brainfacts.org/Thinking.../Smell/.../Making-Sense-of-Scents-Smell-and-the-Brain by Allison Marin (Curley) and Leslie Vosshall, Phd Vosshall Lab, Laboratory Laboratory of Neurogenetics and Behaviour, Rockefeller University, 27 January 2015.

Appendix: Further or recommended reading

Here you will find additional books, resources and websites. This list is by no means comprehensive, as the fields in question are rich in resources. This is a just a sample list to help you begin your explorations.

Author resources:

Savour: an eight-week journey of the senses by Karyn Prentice. My free ebook to download, available at **www.fletcherprentice.com/resources**

Part 1

A Five Season card deck of 25 cards illustrating all five seasons, with the essence and qualities of each season listed on the back of each card. There are practices and reflective questions to bring the five seasons and the five elements to life. See **www.fletcherpentice.com/resources**

Websites and online resources

www.gratefulness.org for inspiration about developing a gratitude practice, poems, a place to light a candle for someone and much more.

www.inspiration.com/visual-learning/mind-mapping for mind mapping tips.

Further reading

Part 1

Ackerman D. (1990). *A Natural History of the Senses*. London, Chapman Publishers.

Brown B. (2010). *The Gifts of Imperfection: Let Go of Who You Think You're Supposed to be and Embrace Who You Are. Your Guide to Wholehearted Living*. Minnesota, Hazelden.

Brown B. (2012). *Daring Greatly: How the Courage to Be Vulnerable Transforms the Way We Live, Love, Parent and Lead*. London, Penguin.

Cameron J. (1994). *The Artist's Way: A Course on Discovering Your Creative Self*. London, Pan.

Cameron J. (2016). *It's Never Too Late to Begin Again: Discovering Creativity and Meaning at Midlife and Beyond*. New York, Tarcher Perigree.

Ford A. (2011). *The Art of Mindful Walking.* East Sussex, Leaping Hare Press.

Fredrickson B. (2014). *Love 2:0.* New York, Penguin.

Gilbert D. (2007). *Stumbling on Happiness.* USA, Harper Perennial New Ed edition.

Gilbert E. (2015). *Big Magic: Creative Living Beyond Fear*. London, Bloomsbury Publishing.

Hanson R. (2011). *Just One Thing*. California, New Harbinger Publications.

Harris M. (2017). *Solitude: in Pursuit of a Singular Life in a Crowded World*. London, Random House.

Harrison M. (ed). *Four Volumes: Spring, Summer, Autumn, Winter.* London, Elliott & Thompson.

Hershey T. (2015). *Sanctuary: Creating a Space for Grace in Your Life*. Chicago, Loyola Press.

Kunditz D. (1998). *Stopping: How to Be Still When You Have to Keep Going*. California, Conari Press.

Magill SP. (2006). *Fully Human*. Washington, Balcladdoch Press.

O'Donohue J. (2015). *Walking in Wonder: Eternal Wisdom for a Modern World*. New York, Crown Publishers.

Patterson E. (2019). *Reflect to Create*. London, The Centre for Reflection and Creativity.

Peck A. (2016). *Be More Tree*. London, CICO Books.

Penman D. (2015). *Mindfulness for Creativity: Adapt, Create and Thrive in a Frantic World*. London, Piatkus.

Quadrille (2018). *Scratch Off, 50 Ways to Slow Down Diary*. Quadrille Publishing Ltd.

Read M. (2014). *Slowing Down in a Speed Stressed World*. USA, Life Press.

Salzburg S. (2002). *Loving Kindness: The Revolutionary Art of Happiness*. Massachusetts, Shambhala Publications.

Siegel D. (2010). *Mindsight: Transform Your Brain with the New Science of Kindness*. London, Oneworld Publications.

Somers B., Gordon-Brown I., Marshall H. (2002).*Journey in Depth*. Cropston, Archive.

Sunim H., Kim C-Y. (2018). *The Things You Can See Only When You Slow Down*. London, Penguin.

Whyte D. (2001). *Crossing the Unknown Sea: Work as a Pilgrimage of Identity*. New York, Riverhead Books.

Wohlleben P. (2015). *The Hidden Life of Trees*. London, Harper Collins.

Part 2

Anderton-Swain P. (2016). *Gardening Tips for the Soul*. Create Space UK, Amazon.

Balles T. (2004). *Dancing With The Ten Thousand Things: Ways to Become a Powerful Healing Presence.* iUniverse

Cardillo J. (2013). *The Five Seasons*. New Jersey, New Page Books.

Gooley, T. (2015). *The Walker's Guide to Outdoor Clues & Signs*. London, Sceptre.

Hershey T. (2009). *The Power of Pause*. Chicago, Loyola Press.

Hershey T. (2015). *Sanctuary*. Chicago, Loyola Press.

Holder, J. (2013). *49 Ways to Write Yourself Better*. UK, Step Beach Press.

Kunitz S., Lentine G. (2005). *The Wild Braid*. New York, WW Norton & Company.

McClelland C L. (1998). *The Seasons of Change*. California, Conari Press.

Rickman C. (2013). *The Flourish Handbook*. Create Space UK, Amazon.

Search G. (2001). *The Healing Garden: Gardening for the Mind, Body and Soul*. London, BBC World Wide Ltd.

Smith B., Robinson T. (2018). *Slow Down and Grow Something*. Sydney, Murdoch Books.

Sorin F. (2016). *Digging Deep: Unearthing Your Creative Roots Through Gardening*. Philadelphia, Braided Worlds Publishing.

Suzuki, D. (1997). *The Sacred Balance*. London, Bantam Books.

Suzuki, D. & Grady, W. (2004). *Tree A Life Story*. Vancouver, Greystone Books.

Thompson MR. (2014). *Reclaiming the Wild Soul*. Oregon, White Cloud Press.

You might also like to discover:

www.wildlifetrusts.org

There are 45 Wildlife Trusts across the UK. Consider joining your local Wildlife Trust to learn more about the local reserves, walks, talks and opportunities to support your local green spaces.

www.plantlife.org

Plantlife supports wildflowers, plants and fungi through conservation work in over 4500 acres of nature in England, Scotland and Wales. They are part of the global strategy for plant conservation and are part of Planta Europe, a network of 60 wild plant conservation organisations.

www.parktrust.org

The National Park Trust is a US land conservancy and environmental education non profit dedicated to preserving parks today and creating park stewards for tomorrow across the whole United States.

www.forbes.com/sites/lauramanske/2018/10/20/13-ways-to-enjoy-the-most-beautiful-gardens-in-the-usa-year-round/

Public accessible gardens are abundant across the United States. Here is a glimpse of 13 of them to visit, whatever the season.

Whatever country you live in, look for ways to support nature and the landscape on a bigger scale around you, for you, your loved ones, and as a legacy for all.

Harvest Timing

The apples are gathered in now
And it was a good crop.
The last of the raspberries
Mould on the canes,
A few tomatoes linger
In hopes of one more sunny day.

It's been a good garden year.
I've spent more time than ever
Weeding beds, mowing, trimming;
I even attached the blackberries
And morning glory vines.

Weeks ago I noticed progress in
My cleaning out, but yesterday
I saw these last ones
Have not given up.
New vines, even in September,
Creep back into the walks,
Set off new shoots into the
Rhododendrons.

Now I see life in a mix of ripe fruit
And work that isn't done.
Come Spring, I'll hit the vines again
And feel I've made more progress-
Once more cutting back the
overgrowth
Pulling up the morning glory
Secretly invading the vegetables.
Every year I cut them back.
Sad they in turn grow more.
Life, then, is as much about
The weeds as it are about the fruit.
As ministers, stewards of the
garden.
We weed and prune.
Sometimes getting what we want.
The cuttings, handled well,
Turn to compost for growing
More sweet fruit.

Samuel P. Magill, *Fully Human*

ACKNOWLEDGMENTS

This book would not have come into being were it not for two people: Jackee Holder, who first believed that I could turn my eloquence into written words on the page and helped me hone my craft even when it was tough going; and Elaine Patterson, fellow writer, soul sister and creative partner in our professional life, who has been a stellar support in this project. I am blessed in this work we do together. Her generosity and positive support have been inspirational.

No book becomes itself without an exceptional editor and a gifted designer. Diane Parker has been a tremendous help in supporting the process of expressing my ideas clearly and helping my writing appear on the page as I would wish it to be with an uncanny, intuitive sense of the subject: just the right thing in the right place. I was thrilled she would work with me and it has made all the difference. I also want to thank Andy Meaden who has taken the manuscript and created something that invites the reader to touch the pages, read on and engage with the contents in all its Technicolor glory. His patient and imaginative thinking have been very much appreciated. Thank you to both of you.

My inspiration for this book has to include Sam Magill, my fellow coach and co-teacher who opened the door to me to discover the fifth season, by introducing me through his exquisite work to the bounty of coaching with the seasons in mind. I knew way back then working with the five seasons was made for me and nothing would hold me back after that. This book is the harvest of that.

Thank you also to Monica Ross, Lynne De Lay, Edna Murdoch and Natasha Carlish for reading and commenting on my work and being positive supporters of the project. I can't be too grateful.

I can't finish these acknowledgments without a solemn bow of gratitude for Mother Nature herself; for the hours of walking with clients in parks and gardens, where she would without fail inform, delight, guide, surprise, contain and mirror the conversations we had. The backdrop of landscape and nature has been the greatest teacher of all.

Finally, but never least, is the gardener of my heart who has taught me everything about gardens, patience and love and what it means to be utterly at peace in nature. Thank you Peter, from the bottom of my heart for your example, for putting up with long stretches of me writing during our holidays, my grumpiness and impatience with myself, and for unfailingly looking after me whilst I planted my heart and soul into these pages. This book is dedicated to you.

"with freedom, books, flowers and the moon,
who could not be happy?"

Oscar Wilde

Lightning Source UK Ltd.
Milton Keynes UK
UKHW051326050720
365988UK00008B/378